Discipleship Books:

Humility

By

Philip Watson

Dedication

Dedicated to my loving wife Dianne, and my three children, Andrew, Jonathon and Ruth.

My grateful thanks for allowing me to spend so much of my spare time writing these words.

Acknowledgments

My grateful thanks to Warren Portsmouth who patiently helped me review the manuscripts of my books. Warren suggested improvements and asked questions at appropriate points.

I also want to acknowledge the help of the Holy Spirit for inspiring me to write these books and for frequently reminding me of scriptures, relevant to topics, in each book.

Books about Jesus:

> He Changed Our World
> The Ministry of Jesus
> The Incarnation
> The Son
> Attitude In Jesus' Teachings (soon to be published)

Other books written by Philip Watson:

> Humility
> Great Summaries
> 80 Spiritual Principles

Books Coming Soon

> 1200 Great Quotes
> Attitude In the Old Testament
> Attitude In Acts, Epistles and Revelation
> Evidence The Bible Is True
> Creation or Evolution
> The Father

Table of Contents

1: The work-load of the leader was so great
that they did not have time to spend with their

Introduction

If there was a chart that registered the most popular subjects Christians liked to read about, most likely, near the top would be subjects like:

- Fulfil your God-given potential.
- Success
- How I changed my world
- Being an over-comer

And near the bottom of that chart:

- Repentance.
- Fasting.
- Discipline.
- Humility!

Most Christians would 'like' to be able to tick the top four boxes while most of us try avoid the bottom four – which are the ones, we probably, need the most - to make us effective and well rounded, Christians.

So why do we avoid the bottom ranked subjects, including humility? There are probably a number of reasons, including; many of us have brought into the consumer mentality of our modern age; and have applied that mentality, to our faith and then, asked. "What is in this for me", rather than. "What will make me of more benefit to others – and to the kingdom of God?"

Another reason the subject of humility may be avoided; we do not understand what the word means. What the word means in the (original) Greek language, is unpacked in chapter 2 and perhaps there is another reason for avoiding the subject. Some Christians may think negatively and think that anyone writing about the subject of humility, is likely to suggest that a truly humble person is someone who is willing to walk many miles/km on their knees - or that humility means, saying to ourselves, "I am nothing!" Neither of those suggestions is found in these pages.

The question, 'why is humility important' is the subject of the first chapter but to drop a few hints about what is in that chapter? If the Father/Son and Holy Spirit did not exist, we would not need humility. If there were no other people on the face of the Earth, we would not need humility. It might be of use if we lived alone on a desert Island, and then only humility if we were honest with ourselves, about any mistakes we had made. However; as it is likely that most readers (most likely all readers) live and relate to other people so they will find a study of humility beneficial if they want to successfully relate to:Other people.

- The Father, Son and Holy Spirit.

Humility is not a minor subject in the Bible. Humility and it's derivative words *humble, humbles, humbled* and *humbly* are found 98 times in the Bible, while the opposite of humility, pride, is also mentioned frequently throughout the Bible. The word *pride* (69 times), *proud* (44 times) and *proudly* (3 times).

Humility is a quality that the Father, the Son, and Holy Spirit *look for*, in human beings. Jesus said that

> "whoever humbles himself isgreatest in the kingdom of God."
> Matt 18:4

The Apostle James wrote.

> "God opposes the proud (the opposite of being humble) but gives grace to the humble." James 4:6 (N.I.V)

One meaning of the word grace is *favour* - implying that the Father and the Son, *look* for people with humble hearts, and when they see that quality, they say to themselves. I can do business with that person. I will give 'favour' to that person. That is why the author of the book of Numbers wrote about one of the greatest leaders in the Old Testament,

> "Now Moses was a very humble man...." Num 12:3

Another person who stands out in the Bible as a person with a humble heart; was Mary - the mother of Jesus. Her humble attitude is almost certainly the reason God selected her

to be the mother of Jesus. We can detect Mary's humble attitude in her response to the angel Gabriel after he told her that she would conceive a child who would be, God's son. She said, "I am the Lord's servant....Luke 1:38

In every age; the Father, Son and Holy Spirit scan the globe, for people they can do business with. People they know they can use as instruments to extend the kingdom of God;

on this Earth!

I wrote this book as much for myself as for readers, for I have long believed that Christians should feel *good* about being the unique person they are, the one God has created them to be. Further, that He loves each of us, more than words can ever, convey. I also believe that as Christians, we should endeavour to climb every hill or mountain that is in front of us. Face the challenges all of us encounter, from time to time.

I fervently believe that Christians should use the talents they have. The training they have received, and their experiences of life for; the benefit of others and for the sake of the kingdom of God.

Or in few words, Christians will ideally be people who live life to the full, respecting their own worth, the worth of others and the

 kingdom of God!

And yet I wondered, is it possible to live a full life. To face every challenge, life throws at us. Enjoy being the unique person God created us to be. To love ourselves. To use every talent we have and training we have received; and still be a humble person? Or to put that question; more simply.

Can you and I live life to the full, without being full of ourselves?

The correct understanding of the meaning of the word *humility*, plays a big part in the answer to that question and the meaning of the Greek word ...., will play a pivotal role in this book about humility . Someone who is full of themselves is usually a proud person. Once I began writing this book, the word *pride* – came up quite naturally. Pride comes in for bad press throughout the Bible, and yet I wondered; is there a good pride?

Then there is 'false humility'. False humility is seldom mentioned in the Bible but where we find examples of false humility. God; in Moses case, and the Angel of the Lord in Gideon's case; become 'very' impatient with both of those men , when they tried to say, in as many words. I am not worthy of nor, capable of, the task I am being asked to do.

So with even a basic knowledge of the Bible, it appears that *humility* is in – and *false humility* and *pride* are out. But is there a healthy pride and what about loving yourself as Jesus urged his followers to do? Matt 22:39

Hopefully this book will answer all those questions and help distinguish between pride and loving yourself. But more importantly; identify ways we can:

- apply the oil of humility to so many areas of our lives,
- making our life more successful, and
- help; others enjoy their relationship with us, and we with them.

A word for some readers. This book is 'not' written for those who are really struggling with their self-esteem. If you as a reader, are struggling to feel good about yourself and love yourself, then perhaps a book or a sermon about how valuable you are; is the right book for you, at this time. Once that message about your incredible worth is established in your mind/soul and spirit – and you beginning to want to soar; then come and read this book.

Chapter 1

Is Humility Important

"Do we need humility?" is a good question to ask, and the answer depends on who you are. If someone is a disciple of Jesus, then humility is essential, from day one. Following on are some reasons why we need humility, if we are to be a successful disciple of Jesus.

Our relationship with the Father, Son and Holy Spirit

The Father

The Bible is a book that invites readers, to 'walk with God'. E.g. Micah 6:8 One condition of that walk, is that people walk 'humbly' with God - the problem being, many adults want to live independently of God and/or, anyone else. That desire to live independently of God, is typified by the words I saw on a sign. The words on the sign, invited those reading the sign, to come to philosophy lectures. The key words were,

LEARN HOW TO THINK, NOT WHAT TO THINK.

In other words, come to the lectures and we will teach you how to think-independently of any other person or religion. There is an implicit pride; in this independent way of thinking that assumes past or collective wisdom; can play no part in determining, today's decisions.

By contrast, the committed Christian is a person who has humbled herself or himself; and said. "I am going to live God's ways because I believe that living by God's values; is by far the best choice! If I choose to live by my values - ultimately my limited insights will lead to a fools paradise - in which I may 'think' I have found life – but in fact, my life will fall short of - real life. The key factors in those respective choices are, pride and humility. Pride says "my way" while humility says, "God's way!"

Through the words that can be found In the

book of Proverbs, King Solomon appeals to readers to; acknowledge God's greater knowledge, insight and wisdom and place their trust in his superior; knowledge, insight and wisdom.

> "Trust in the Lord
> With all your heart
> Lean not into your own understanding.
> In all your ways acknowledge Him,
> And he will make your paths straight."
> Prov 3:5&6

To trust in God implies that He is 'trustworthy'. To trust with 'all' your heart implies that God is, totally trustworthy. In the middle line of those verses, Solomon wrote.

> *"Lean not into your own understanding".*

Solomon did not mean, do not have any understanding or information of your own, but recommends that we lean towards what we believe is God's view, and God's insight. The fourth line invites us to seek God's guidance in 'every' situation. That invitation implies that, God 'knows' about, 'every' situation. Finally in the fifth line there is a promise, he will make straight your paths or as the Good News Bible renders these words - 'and he will show you the right way'.

It is amazingly that the majority of the human race believe they are more intelligent and wiser than God, and that they have more insight, and consequently - don't need his help or insights, to determine their own pathway in life. The prophet Isaiah offers us reasons why we should trust God.

> *"For my thoughts are not your thoughts,*
> *neither are your ways my ways,*
> *declares the Lord.*
> *As the heavens are higher than the earth,*
> *so are my ways higher than your ways*
> *and my thoughts than your thoughts."*
> Isa 55:8&9

The key word in the two verses above, is the word "higher" which conveys the same concept as an eagle or satellite, viewing the Earth from a much higher perspective, and that higher perspective enables them to see the whole landscape including objects and people that those viewing the same scene, cannot see from a, ground-view perspective.

If that higher (divine) perspective is taken on board, humility is not about belittling ourselves. Rather; it is about being smart enough to acknowledge is that God has a higher perspective and infinitely more of everything.   More   knowledge,   insight, perspective, wisdom e.t.a.

The Son

Humility is not only required for a relationship to God the Father, but also in our relationship to Jesus the Son. The most common title for Jesus in the New Testament, is Lord. If we are Christians, then Jesus is our Lord and that word "Lord", is not meant to be like the title of a person, such as Mr, Mrs, Miss, MS, Sir or Ma'am. It is meant to be much more than that and is epitomised by the saying. "If He is not Lord of all, he is not Lord at all." No one can say "Jesus is my Lord", and mean it - and not have a sense of humility. A humility that based on the understanding that, 'I' am no longer king or queen, of my life. King Jesus is, my Lord.

In our relationship to Jesus, we make him Lord of 'all' our lives, meaning. All that we do, and all that we say, and all that we think should derive from his teachings - his example and the leading of the Holy Spirit.

The Holy Spirit

It is the same with the Holy Spirit. We Christians are blessed in so many ways by the Holy Spirit, but our relationship with the

Holy Spirit is not meant to be a one-way street in which we receive assurance, and blessings and the fruit and gifts of the Holy Spirit. It is meant to be, a two-way street and in that two-way street - we endeavour to listen to what the Spirit is saying to us. In a vision that Jesus gave to the Apostle John, he repeatedly urged the Churches (named in the first three chapters of the book of Revelation) to, "Listen to what the Spirit is saying to the Churches."

Listening to what the Spirit is saying means, we acknowledge that the Holy Spirit has identified some task in the kingdom of God, for us to do. It may be a very small task or it may be a large task – the size is not the issue. When the Holy Spirit prompts us to do a task;

it is because he has seen a need that we may not be aware of, and he wants us to be Jesus, in a particular situation.

Kingdom of Heaven/God

The terms, kingdom of heaven and kingdom of God; are often used interchangeably in the Bible. The kingdom of heaven includes every activity that normally takes place in a church – but also every word or action by any Christian, anywhere, away from the Church. Any word or action that brings the love or truth of the king, into a situation. That situation could be in your home or at the beach or in an office or factory or farm – anywhere people are.

Jesus spoke these words and about entering the kingdom of heaven; and becoming great in it.

> "I tell you the truth, unless you change and become like little children, you will never enter the kingdom of heaven. Therefore, whoever humbles himself like this child is the greatest in the kingdom of heaven." Matt 18:3-4 (N.I.V)

Humility is required in the kingdom of God because every is Christian is asked to consider them self as, and to be - a servant – just like Jesus was.

Christian World view

In the Christian world- view; everything is a *gift.*

- Eternal life is a gift.
- Life is a gift.
- Our spirit is a gift.
- Our talents are gifts.
- Our leaders, are gifts.

- Faith is a gift.
- Holy Spirit is a gift.
- There are gifts of the Spirit.
- The fruit of the Spirit – are gifts in the sense that we do not buy them.
- Our salvation is a gift.
- Our works are pre planned.

In a few words,

we Christians are, gift recipients.

So because virtually everything in life and our spiritual life is a gift, we cannot boast about having earned or deserved, anything. The Apostle Paul summarised the situation in his letter to the Church at Rome,

"For from him are all things..." Rom 11:39

Further, in the Christian world view, my/your possessions and money do not belong to us. Rather in that view, we have been entrusted with them, like stewards or caretakers. In that world-view, we regard our money, our possessions and time, as ultimately belonging to God. When we fill out insurance forms for an insurance company to insure our home and contents car and other items. In the box where you and I owners would be expected to fill our name – instead of our name - we really should put the name of 'God' in the box, as the owner of our car, possessions, house e.t.a. and our name as steward.

Humility as an oil in our human relationships

Not only is humility a vital key, in our relationships with The Father, The Son and The Holy Spirit. Humility can be one of the keys to successful relationships, with other people. Whether these relationships are with people in our home; our work, our place of study, our Church, or social club or sports group. Basically, where-ever and however, people meet. Rick Warren, Senior pastor of the large, Willow Creek Church, wrote,

> *"Humility is an oil that helps soothe and smooth every human relationship."*

Notice the words 'every'. Imagine every human relationship we have being impacted for good, if only we have that one quality – humility!

Humility's opposite-number pride; and is a significant factor in damaging, any and every relationship we have. Relationships with friends. With work mates/colleagues. Our employer or employees. Our parents, our children. Our wife or husband. All these relationships benefit from the oil of humility and are harmed, by pride.

Bible teacher, Joyce Meyer wrote about the way she and her husband Dave, apply humility to their marriage relationship. When it became obvious they were disagreeing over some issue, instead of digging in their heels, over the issue and insisting they were right - and the other wrong, they begin to use words that indicate some humility. "I think I am right, but I may be wrong." P23 Conflict Free Living (Charisma House)

That sort of humility, does, wonders for a marriage relationship, and any human relationship. If that type of humility was brought to every disagreement, it will lead to deeper bonds, because both partners will recognise that over the course of time. One partner is likely to be right about 50% of the time, and the other partner, also 50%. And it does not matter if the figures are 60/40 in favour of one partner. Humility does not keep a record of the score.

There are two natural partners to humility - 'truth' and 'honesty'. The truth is, sometimes we will be right and the truth is; sometimes we will be wrong. Or as is sometimes the case. We may be, partially right, and the other person partly right, also. So in allowing for the fact that we may be wrong in a particular situation, we are only being honest with ourselves and others, and that honesty usually results in us, going higher, in the other person's estimation.

We may go higher in our 'own' estimation if insist we are right most of the time but if we want to go higher in the estimation of other people; then we will make allowance for the fact that we may be wrong sometimes. And that acknowledgement that we may be wrong sometimes; is going to gain us enormous credits, with every person we are in relationship with.

Rob Parsons wrote in his book *Loving Against The Odds,*

> *Great marriages are not made by two good lovers but two good forgivers.*

That formula for a successful marriage, seems to be a contrast to the, Hollywood formula. That Hollywood formula (as conveyed by movies) seems to be that 'two good lovers' is the best way for a happy and successful relationship. But it seems to me; that every time I pick up magazines with articles about Hollywood couples, the movie stars are in some sort of bitter dispute with one another. And often, lawyers are involved.

So the formula suggested by Rob Parsons, two great forgivers is most likely the answer! To forgive, requires humility. Humility allows for the fact that the other party could have made a mistake or that we could have made a mistake. When one, or preferably 'both' parties admit they have made mistakes or may be wrong, then disagreements usually, dissolve quickly. And I suggest, forgiving the other person in a marriage (or any relationship) is usually the gateway to a great relationship, and I suggest – to them being - two great lovers.

The idea that 'we' also, may also have our faults and may have spoken words we later regret, is backed up by what Jesus said:

> "Why do you look at the speck of sawdust in your brother's eye (read – the other persons eyes) and not look at the plank in your own eye?" Matt 7:3 (N.I.V)

In other words, if we recognise that we 'too' can be wrong, it is much easier to forgive.

Pride sees whole plank in the other person's eyes (the person we are disagreeing with) and considers e we only have, merely, a speck.

Others gifts

Humility unlocks the doors to a better relationships with other people, in other ways. Humility allows us to focus on the gifts, skills and training; that others have. Over the years I have gathered enough quotes for a book called '1200 Great Quotes'. (yet to be published). In this book, apart from about a dozen quotes of my own, all the rest are from nearly 500 Christians.

During the task of collecting those 1200 Great Quotes, I had the chance to evaluate the writings and teachings of many different Christians. During that long task, I often found myself, thanking God for raising in His kingdom, so many gifted writers and preachers and teachers. Those authors/speakers whose quotes I have recorded, seemed to have the ability to put into easily understood words, truths about a great variety of subjects. And they did so in a way that was superior to what, I could never come up with.

Humility is not about denying our gifts or experience or insights. Humility allows us the room to acknowledge the gifts of others; and rejoice in the gifts, God has given them. Being humble, means we can honour God for the gifts, training and experience we have, while at the same time we can honour others for the gifts, training and experience, they have. Nancy Missler wrote.

> "Humility is the ability to see ourselves as we truly are, which then leaves us free to get excited about the triumphs of others and love them as God desires." p184 Private Worship.

Chapter 2

What is Humility

What is humility? Does being humble mean, falling on the floor before God, not daring to, even look up? Living in a desert monastery? Serving on the door at Church? Those actions might be signs of a humble person. What is important; is the meaning of the word. There are two key aspects, to the Greek word *Tapeinophrosyne* - from which we get the English word, humility

The first part of the explanation of the word *Tapeinophrosyne*; is "...lowliness of mind, the estimation of ourselves as insignificant." In the Old Testament, when people wanted to show their humility, their shame or their helplessness; usually they put on clothes made of sack-cloth and put ashes on their heads.

A person who displayed that type of humility was, King Jehoshaphat. When told that his kingdom was surrounded by a vast number of enemies, intent on destroying his kingdom, he went to the Temple in sack-cloth (the roughest from of clothing) and sought God's help. The final words of his prayer, were.

> *"We do not know what to do, but our eyes are upon you." 2 Chron 20:12 (N.I.V)*

Both through by his actions and words, Jehosaphat showed humility and admitted he needed God's help.

By contrast to King Jehosaphat, other kings of Israel and Judah, when they faced the same over-whelming odds; acted very differently. Perhaps they reasoned. I have not sought God's help in the day to day running of my kingdom, so I will not humble myself now, and turn to him for help. So they tried strengthening their defences and forming last-minute military alliances or buying off the enemy, as ways out of their troubles. Anything, but seeking God's help.

There is a second part to the explanation of

the Greek word *Tapeinophrosyne*. That is;

> *inasmuch as we are so, the correct estimate of ourselves.*

The second part of the meaning of the word *Tapeinophrosyne,* will be the main focus of this book. According to that definition of humility, we should never put ourselves down. Or minimise our skills and talents and training and experience. In fact a 'humble' person who has a *correct estimate of themselves* will say to them self.

> "I have these skills (and list them)"
> "I have this training (and list any training)"
> "I have these qualifications (and list them)"
> "I have this experience (and list it)".

They will also say to themselves. I am important because I am a child of God. I love myself, and there are others who love me – for that is what the definition of humility means - inasmuch as we are so, the correct estimate of ourselves.

The other side of that *correct estimate of ourselves*, is that we will admit that we do not know everything, and therefore sometimes need to ask others for advice. That sometimes we will make mistakes, and continue to make mistakes, though hopefully not the same ones. That sometimes we will think we are right and say so, and then find that we are wrong.

A correct estimate of ourselves will mean that sometimes we will want to do something a particular way (and obviously think it is the best way) while someone else may want to do the same task, another way. And if the task is done the way the other person wants it done, sometimes we will find that the way they suggested; was as good, or even better than, the way we suggested.

Or even if a task is done 'our way', which proves to be the best way. The humble person will not 'crow' about their superior insights because they will remember that in the past, there were occasions when they suggested doing something 'their' way, and that proved to be the wrong way or the less, desirable way.

A key to successful relationships with others, is to have a humble approach when it becomes obvious, others; are wrong. If we are gracious on those occasions when others wrong, they are much more likely to offer the same graciousness, when we make a bad call. Peter Marshall, former chaplain to the U. S Senate prayed.

> "Lord, make us humble when we
> are right, and gracious when others
> are wrong."

Humility in Church

Humility is also found in those who recognise they are not perfect. I like this quote from Rick Warren, senior Pastor of a large Church in the United States, and one I suggest, every Church should have.

> "No perfect people need apply. This
> is a place for those who admit they
> are sinners, need grace and want
> to grow."

The attitude of humility implicit in the statement by Pastor Rick Warren; is an attitude that we ought to bring to our relationships with our fellow Christians in his best selling book *The Purpose Driven Life*.

> "The proper dress for fellowship is
> humility." p148 (Zondervan)

Fellowship is something, deeper than greeting

fellow Christians. Fellowship occurs, when Christians begin to share their lives. Their hopes, their dreams and their goals. True fellowship occurs when we also allow others, to see our weaknesses.

The late, Dr Derek Prince wrote. "Somebody has said that fellowship is "Roof off, walls down". " Most of us don't mind getting the roof off with God and Jesus, because they see through the roof anyway, but most of us get pretty uncomfortable when we let the walls down, so our fellow Christians can see in."

It is in that type of relationship, where real fellowship takes place, and when that type of fellowship takes place; there is a richness in our relationships; far deeper than if we all maintain the outward appearance of, having it all together. Amongst the things humility helps us do, is:

- Admit we make mistakes
- Admit we have faults
- Admit we are sinners (and will continue to sin and fall short of God's perfect standards, till we die)
- Admit to ourselves we are wrong
- Admit to others we are wrong
- Admit we have a problem, when we have one

- Admit that someone in our family has a serious problem
- Admit we don't know the answer to a particular problem
- Admit we don't know the answer to a question about the faith
- Admit that sometimes we get guidance wrong
- Acknowledge that others may have better gifts, talent, training or experience

Are willing to:

- Be led by others
- Receive advice from others
- Receive praise, thanks, compliments from others
- Receive gifts, money or help from others
- Laugh at ourselves because. We 'all' make mistakes and we 'all' have faults.

Being open to admit we have weaknesses, or have made mistakes or have sinned - or whatever, does not mean we have to go to the other extreme, and every time we go a Church group and turn it into a time of, admit every weakness or mistake or sin – but sometimes we may choose to.

In a healthy Church group, Christians will be able to honest with their fellow Christians about any area of life they may be struggling with. For example, a few years ago I joined a firm and in a short space of time, crashed their vehicle, three times! Each occasion it was, my fault!

I came to the new firm, with very good recommendations and a great driving record from the previous firm. By the time I had the third crash, any reputation I had come with, was in tatters; and I was strongly tempted to resign - but we felt that this was a job I was meant to have, after shifting cities.

After the third crash, with good reason, the firm was reviewing my continued employment, and I was under a cloud because there was no one else, I could blame. After the third crash, there was an opportunity in church, to pray for each other about any issue so I asked those nearby to pray for me. To pray about the situation. For a resolution of the problem and for wisdom.

In answer to that prayer, I reviewed 'why' each crash had occurred and it dawned on me that the 'real' reason for all three crashes was because of my 'go, go, go' life-style – a life-style, I was very proud of! I was 'proud' of the way I could achieve so much in each day.

Pride (the opposite of humility) had crept into my life on the back of a very good desire. A desire to make the maximum use, of each day.

NB After identifying the real reason for the series of crashes, I have not had a crash since and with the benefit of hindsight, believe God allowed me to have those three crashes; so that I would recognise my pride. The situation forced me to humble myself and admit to my fellow Christians I was on thin ice at work; and not sure what to do.

A subject I will return to later in the book; is that pride often leads to crashes of some kind, not just in vehicles; but in other areas of our life; if we allow it to creep in.

Humility, and being in the presence of caring Christians, allow us to admit our weaknesses or sins or errors to our fellow Christians and ask for their prayer support – rather than just pretend, everything is OK!

The Apostle Paul wrote in a similar vein to what both what Rick Warren and Derek Prince wrote.

> " *Therefore as God's chosen people....clothe yourselves with compassion, kindness, humility,*

> *gentleness and patience. Bear with each other and forgive whatever grievances you may have against one another...." Col 3:12-13 (N.I.V)*

Sometimes God will allow circumstances to humble us but he would prefer that 'we' clothe ourselves with humility.

Humility is a pre-determined mind-set. A mindset that that we can choose to bring with us, to any time of fellowship, and just as importantly. be something we should take home with us after the time of fellowship; and be an oil that can apply to every relationships with every person we meet, or work with.

False Humility

Pride comes in for bad press in the Bible, but so does, false-humility. An obvious example of false humility, was Moses. At the burning bush, when God commanded Moses to go to the Pharaoh and lead the Israelites out of Egypt, Moses began a litany of excuses including.

> "Who am I?"
> "I have never been eloquent,"....
> "I am slow of speech and tongue."
> "O Lord, please send someone else to do it." etc.

After the last excuse, Genesis chapter four reads:

> "Then the Lord's anger burned against Moses....."

Moses was reprimanded by God because he tried to talk his way out of a task that God had asked him to do. It is implicit in the conversation, that.

- God would not have asked Moses; if He did not think he could do it.
- God would go with him to support him.

The four excuses Moses came up with, were just about the only four, anyone could come up with. There was no use Moses saying to God, "I do not have the time". Effectively the four were

1. I do not have the ability for the task. i.e. I am not eloquent
2. What ability I do have, is not up to the task. i.e. I am slow of speech
3. I am a nobody
4. Someone else would be better suited to the task.

Moses *could* have come up with a number of reasons why he should have said, "yes" on the spot.

- God considers me the perfect man for

> the job otherwise he wouldn't have asked me.
> - God will go ahead, with me
> - God knows I love my people. Unfortunately I expressed that love (many years ago) in the wrong way - by killing an Egyptian who was mistreating one of my people. But he has allowed me time to cool off in the desert, and learn patience over 40 years; herding, dumb sheep.
> - He also knows that I know court procedure and etiquette, because I was raised in the court of a Pharaoh.
> - Unlike the rest of my people. God has recognised that I am familiar this part of the World, presumably through which; I will lead the Hebrew people through, on their way to the Promised land.

Those were five obvious reasons why, Moses should have said, "yes". Moses reluctance, even though he was perfectly suited for the job; is in complete contrast to another person in the Bible who; like Moses was offered a high position; but unlike Moses - accepted on the spot and unlike Moses - had none of the appropriate qualifications for the job. I am referring to Joseph.

Joseph did not have the false-humility of Moses. When he received a dream in which he saw his brothers bowing down to him, he did not hide it, but told his brothers, and also told his father. Understandably, when he told his older brothers about that dream, it went down like a lead balloon.

We can see that Joseph did not have false humility, for when the Pharaoh suggested promoting him to the second most powerful person in the land, *on the spot*. Joseph did not say. "I am sorry Pharaoh, but I am not worthy for this position! There are many reasons why I am unworthy.

- I am the youngest of my brothers.
- I am merely a step brother, to the eldest ten brothers.
- I am a foreigner.
- Egyptian is my second language and not my first.
- While in prison, I learned bad language.
- I do not know court etiquette!
- I have no administrative experience.
- My work history up till now, makes me totally unsuitable for the job of the second most powerful person in Egypt/deputy Pharaoh.

- My C.V. reads:

- *Shepherd (the lowest job in Egyptian eyes because shepherds would sleep with their sheep at night; and consequently, stink)*
- *Slave*
- *servant*
- *Prisoner.*

So you can see Mr Pharaoh, there are ten reasons why, I am totally unsuited for job of - the top administrator, in Egypt."

Joseph could have made a really good case that he was unsuitable for the job based on his work record and experience. Instead, he accepted the position, and took the responsibility seriously. Perhaps he thought. God has so obviously arranged this offer of the second most powerful person in Egypt. Because God has arranged this; I will accept the position. Apparently there is still a canal in Egypt that they call, Joseph's canal.

In the parable of the talents, Jesus is severe on those who do not use their talents to make more money. Even though the word "talent" in the parable refers to a measure of money, if we take Jesus words to refer to what the English language word 'talent', means; we get the same meaning. Jesus message to us and every disciple, is a word of encouragement. Use your talents, rather than bury them, with false humility.

To wrap this chapter, up. The Bible is for humility but against; false-humility. We will exercise humility but not, false-humility if we take on board the meaning of the word; *Tapeinophrosyne*.

 inasmuch as we are so, the correct estimate of ourselves.

Ideally then, the Christian will be a person who does not consider any task beneath them (for that is humility) and at the same time. Not consider any task too great; for that would be (false-humility).

Chapter 3

Humbling Experiences

Not many people will say, "I welcome humbling experiences" but as I look at the value of humility and the damage that pride does, I am sure that humbling experiences do us all, so much good – particularly if we are serious about being, effective as a disciple of Jesus.

If Pastor Tong had written this book, he would probably would have written

> "Dear Lord, please give, 'all' the readers, many humbling experiences!"

To explain the reference to Pastor Tong. Decades ago, when the church in China was actively persecuted, Pastor Tong, came to our Church to talk about how, in spite of, and because of; the persecution - the Church in China grew – about twenty-fold. When we heard him talk about that persecution; naturally we thought. 'How terrible' – and resolved to pray, that God would lessen the persecution, so it was to our enormous surprise, when he said

> "Don't pray that the persecution will stop..."

I needed a few seconds to process what he was saying because I, like most in the west wanted to pray something like. "Lord, please take away their persecution" or. "Lord, please make their life easier" e.t.a. He continued.

"Don't pray those kinds of prayers, only pray that our backs will be strong enough to bear it – and that we will be faithful".

He said. "Often in the West, Christians pray and ask that God will take away all their troubles, but when we look at the good they do us (like increase our understanding, our patience and cause us to rely on God alone), I should pray that God will, 'increase' your troubles!"

So if Pastor Tong was author of this book, I

imagine he would write. Because humility is so good for Christians, please dear God, give the readers, many humbling experiences, because that will keep them humble and consequently make them much more effective, as disciples of Jesus.

Because Pastor Tong is not author of this book, readers will be spared that prayer, though I suggest that humbling experiences from time to time; are good for us all, because they keep us humble and being humble is such an important part of our Christian clothing. Amongst other things, humbling experiences are an effective way to melt pride and an effective way to create, understanding.

How we handle circumstances that humble us and seem to show us in a bad light, and prick our ego; is the hall-mark of our growth as a Christian. Pride is often evident when we make mistakes and try and cover them up or blame others. The reluctance in most of us, to take full responsibility for our errors, reminds me of a quote from Ed Cole:

> "Maturity does not come with age.
> We are mature (at any age), when
> we begin to take responsibility for
> our actions."

An example in the New Testament of a person who humbled himself when he found himself in humbling circumstances, was the prodigal son. In the parable that Jesus told, when the prodigal son had spent all his father's money on parties and prostitutes; eventually out of desperation; he began a job, feeding pigs - the lowest form of animal in Jewish society. Then, when he came to his senses, he said to himself. The servants in my father's home have a better existence than I have. By that admission, he was not humbling himself, he was just being honest.

> *Honesty is not humility, but is often the doorway to humility.*

Honesty and humility are natural partners, just a pride, has some natural partners; which I will come to in chapter seven. Another natural partner to humility; is grace. The prodigal son's life only started going forward again when he became, honest. Honest with himself. Honest with his family and honest with God.

Once he had became honest with himself, and God, he showed both the humility and maturity to be willing to accept responsibility for his actions; and being prepared to take the long walk home and lose face before his neighbours. Lose face before his father's servants and his extended family - and admit his wrong-doing to his father; and then. Ask to be employed as a servant in his father's house.

While this is only a story, a parable; it is a story that would have spoken to many of those listening. In those times, (and in many cultures today), losing face (humbling ourselves), is almost as bad as dying.

The occasional dose of humbling circumstances does most of us good. Sometimes those humbling circumstances are because we have made a mistake, and then we are forced to admit (again), that we are fallible people. There is a quote of Mother Teresa's which is relevant to this chapter because in that quote she ties sincerity (honesty) with humility, and these with our fallibility or limitations.

> *"Sincerity is nothing but humility and you acquire humility only by accepting your limitations." Mother Teresa*

Everything starts With Prayer p59 (White Cloud Press)

The fact that many people feel embarrassed

or humiliated by their limitations or weaknesses or when they have made a mistake; resonated with a conversation found in one of Rick Joyner's books called the, '*The Call*'. In that book, Rick Joyner claimed that he, like the Apostle John, was taken to heaven. Whether it was his spiritual body that went to heaven or it was in the form of a vision, Rick left open. While in heaven, he had quite a few conversations with Jesus.

One of the loving, but challenging comments Jesus made to Rick while he was in heaven, is relevant to this part of the book. Jesus said,

> *"The humble cannot be embarrassed."*

Those words ("The humble cannot be embarrassed,") are a challenge because I imagine that most readers, are like me; and feel embarrassed or humiliated when we make mistakes. Many people feel embarrassed about the mistakes they have made because their pride, has been hurt?" If that is the case, maybe it is a good thing that our pride has been pricked, because it shows we are living a life based on pride. A pride that is based on - how I/we, appear to others?"

If our life is based on how we appear to

others, we are little different to the Pharisees of Jesus' time – many of whom were concerned with how they appeared to others, particularly about how religious they looked.

Jesus took the pharasees to task about the way they wanted to be 'seen' to be godly. Seen to be fasting and seen to be praying on street corners – so that others, would notice their godly actions.

By contrast, Jesus lived, another way to the Pharisees. A quote about Jesus ministry (from a source I cannot remember) epitomises Jesus' life.

> *'He lived as if he nothing to lose or*
> *gain or hide'.*

Jesus lived as if he had nothing to lose, gain or hide. Because he did not have any pride, he did not have pride, to lose. We can see that in the way he conducted his ministry. He was not embarrassed when a woman with internal bleeding, touched him. He was not embarrassed when foreign women approached him at a well. He was not embarrassed when he put spittle on the eyes of a blind man, or John leaned on his shoulder at the last supper etc.

That is one of the challenges for disciples of Jesus today, from Jesus' life. He lived as if he had nothing to gain, or hide or lose. Jesus lived from the beginning of his ministry as if he was not seeking to gain credits from anyone, while seeking to fulfil God's purposes for his life. If he was seeking to gain credits from others, he would not have said and done, most of the things, he did.

For example. He would not have stopped, to pick up little children. Or stopped to talk with, a (despised) Samaritan woman, at a well. Or, he would not have called, a tax collector (Matthew) to be one of his disciples. Or asked another tax collector (Zaachaeus) , if he could come and dine at his house.

Most readers will not understand the reasons why most of the Jews who were accompanying Jesus would have reacted unfavourably; when they heard Jesus ask if he could come to the house of tax collector called Zaachaeus, for a meal.

To be a tax collector in Jesus time, meant buying a tax-collecting franchise from the Roman authorities. The pay the Romans offered, was minimal, but there was a tacit understanding that a tax collector would, within reason; charge 'extra', above what the Roman authorities required the tax-collector to collect from, each Jewish tax-payer. Because of the extra the tax collectors collected, they were able to make up for the low pay.

In that business, they were a law unto themselves, about how much 'extra', they collected from tax payers, and it seems that many tax collectors made themselves rich. And if any Jewish citizens who did not pay the tax, demanded by the tax collector, could be threatened with a visit from Roman soldiers.

So you can imagine how the average Jew felt towards tax -collectors, like Zaachaeus. One of their 'own' countrymen, had bought a tax-collecting franchise from a foreign, (occupying) power and that franchise enabled them to, 'rip-off' their fellow country men and women. So it is not hard to imagine, why tax collectors were, so despised?

Knowing that background information, it makes it all the more remarkable that Jesus called a tax collector to be one of his followers, and that he invited himself to the house of a tax collector, Zaachaeus. Those two actions of Jesus, emphasize a point already made. That Jesus lived his life as if he had, nothing to. *Lose or hide or gain*. Another way of saying the same thing is.

> *Jesus lived for his mission, not his position.*

What a great way to live. If you or I do not live for prestige, we cannot lose prestige. If pride is not a factor in our thinking, we cannot have our pride dented. If pride is not a factor in anything we say or do, then we are truly free! Free to do or say anything that is for the good of others; or for the sake of the kingdom of God. Some readers may want to pray this prayer.

> *"Lord Jesus, forgive me for my pride. May I be like you; and not concerned about my image; but only about doing God's will and using my gifts and training and experiences - to help others. In your name. Amen."*

Chapter 4

Experiences That Humble

The last chapter was about humbling experiences while this one is about experiences, that humble us.

Humbling experiences are ones that affect us because we are in the middle them; and have to deal with them; either by being humble enough to admit them or alternatively. Try and hide them from others, because we are embarrassed.

This chapter is about experiences that humble us. In these experiences, we are primarily spectators, but they can equally produce humility in us, for our good. These experiences that humble us; usually occur when we see people who seem to have; life against them but act as if, everything in Life was *for* them and the world is, their oyster!

When we see, hear or read about such people, it is always good for us, for they remind us of how much we have, and how fortunate most of us are. In developed countries, we tend to view as a 'major inconvenience' those times when someone spills coffee or some other drink, or that we are suffering great hardship; if because of high building or hills; we cannot get full cell-phone coverage!

What we in developed countries may view as a major inconvenience; in some countries is not a problem at all because the people there cannot afford coffee (let alone from a selection of coffees); or have enough money to buy a cell-phone or T.V. So our frustration at the spilt coffee or the poor cell-phone reception at a particular place; is not a concern to many in the world; because they do not have the luxury of having those things, in the first place.

It is only because, we in developed countries have life, so out of kilter, that these incredibly minor   inconveniences   become,   major inconveniences. What helps keep life in it's proper perspective are those times when I have had experiences that have humbled me – because I have seen or heard about the 'attitude', in people who are, behind the ball; so to speak. Following on are three examples.

The Blind Man

A bus arrives at a bus stop. A man is waiting at the bus-stop, whose head moves back and forth as the bus approaches. He has a white stick. When the bus stops and the doors open, the man first taps the footpath, and then walks towards the open door of the bus. He taps the metal floor of the bus with his stick, then steps onto the bus. He has a plastic card that he uses to pay for his fare. He places the card on top of the electronic machine, which he locates, by feeling for it.

After he has heard the 'beep, beep' of the electronic machine (which indicates a fare has been deducted), he walks down the aisle; grasping lightly the top of each seat in order to keep to the centre of the aisle. After he has felt for a seat that has no-one on it, he sits down and the bus moves off.

The bus had not gone more than 600 yds/meters, when he calls out. "Driver, has the route changed?" In his mind, if the bus was following its 'normal' route, it would go about 400 yds/meters, then (because he had memorised the approximate time the bus travels in a particular direction before taking a turn to the left or right) he would normally hear the engine begin to slow down and he would feel the lurch of the bus as it turned ninety degrees to the left.

He had also memorised that the bus would accelerate briefly after the left turn, and then slow again - then it would turn ninety degrees to the right – if it were following the normal route. But because the bus had not followed that familiar sequence of turns; of de-acceleration and acceleration (a sequence he had memorised) he called out, "driver, has the route changed?"

The driver was somewhat embarrassed that this blind man had picked up the change of route and called out - for he did not feel it was necessary to inform him (a blind man) because he assumed that all the 'sighted' passengers had seen that there were major road-works blocking the normal route and a large sign indicating a detour. The driver assumed that the blind man would be, none the wiser, about the route change!

After the blind man called out, nearby passengers quickly explained the reason for the change of route and the fact that the bus would soon return to the normal route, so the blind man, was put at ease.

Once the bus was back on its' normal route, it carried on in a straight-line for about 1 mile/1600 meters. The blind man, continued to monitor the straight-line progress of the bus, listening to the sound of the engine. He knew, from the sound of the engine and the decrease in speed, when (and if) the bus stopped at any of the three intersections along that 1 mile/1600m stretch of road.

He also monitored through, listening to the sounds the bus made. The sounds the people made, as they exited the bus and the movements of the bus - each time the bus stopped at any of the four bus stops along that, one mile stretch of road.

When the bus finally arrived at the bus station, he got off with all the other passengers and went his way. He did not need to be told, "we are at the bus station now." He knew! It was obvious to him that it was, the bus station, even though he could not see it. That is because he had memorised the sounds and movements the bus and people make when it arrives at the bus station.

i.e. The bus would turn right; then travel in a straight-line for another 400 yds/meters; then; after taking another right turn, the bus would travel approximately another 100 yds/meters in a straight line, before turning into the bus station.

The blind man would also know (from memory) that, when the bus turned into the bus station, the feel of the bus turning; was different from when it turned, say a corner or into a bus-stop. The way the bus would turn into the bus station, would be a wide-arc movement, interspersed by a mild bump, (which was at the entrance to the bus station), and that bump was different from when the bus turned a corner or, pulled into a bus stop.

Another confirmation that he was in the bus station, was that he would sense that the bus was being 'manoeuvred' into a, bus-bay.. That type of movement was different from the type of movement that occurs, when a bus moves into an ordinary bus-stop, on the street. He also knew he was at the bus station for another reason. Apart from the wide arc and the bump, he knew that when the bus was at the bus station, because he could hear the sound of, 'all' the passengers rising out of their seats – rather than just; one or two.

As soon as he was off the bus; he moved away and got on with whatever plans; he had for that day.

Now the question is. Who was the most alert and intuitive person, on that bus? The blind man or the sighted passengers? I hope I do not need to answer that question!

I find it humbling to see men and women like that. People who though they seem disabled to us, do not ask for special considerations or sympathy – and will do every possible activity – apart from those few activities where it is absolutely essential to have sight. People who apart from a few limitations, have a; go, go, go, mentality.

The Westerner

A Christian from the west, enters a hut/home in Africa. The floor of the home, is earth; and the walls are made of sticks and roof is a thatched roof. The woman who owns the house, does all her cooking in one metal pot, over a charcoal fire. The metal pot and cooking spoons; are the only furniture items she owns - apart from a bucket for collecting water, and a broom made of brush wood. She and her children sleep on mats on the floor. The only clothes she has, are those she is wearing.

The Christian (from the west), who went into this home, accepted her hospitality of drink and food. She spoke with great joy of God's goodness to her. The Christian from the west said afterwards, " I wept that a person could be so grateful to God for all his goodness and yet have, by western standards; so little."

I have heard of similar stories of people in the poorer parts of India, where people live in houses that are slightly better than this house in Africa but the people have a similar number of possessions, and their lives are characterised by: laughter, joy, hospitality and gratefulness to God!

I find myself asking. If my possessions consisted to a metal cooking pot, spoon, home-made broom, sleeping mat and one pair of clothes; would I be grateful to God for all his goodness, or endlessly complain to God that he has given me a hard lot in life?

The Spectator

One more example, that I found humbling. I was a spectator at a Commonwealth Games, athletic meeting. These games are attended by countries that were formerly part of the British Empire, and as such, are smaller than the Olympics.

One event I recall clearly from those Games, was the women's 4x100 meter relay final which I viewed from the stand on the opposite side, to the final straight. The Sun that was behind me, so it shone on the athletes as they sprinted down the final straight, towards the finish line.

Heading towards the finishing line were a group of sprinters from traditionally powerful sprinting nations, Australia, Canada, The Bahamas, Jamaica, Nigeria and England. The sprinters of these leading countries were all bunched together. The only exception, was the sprinter from the Fiji. A country with a population of around 500,000 at the time.

When the last runner for the Fiji team took the baton, she was 50 yards behind the rest of the field. At that level, and considering that the other seven teams were all bunched together, it was an embarrassment that her team, was so far behind. In marathon terms, you would have said that her team was, 'miles behind'.

If that female athlete from Fiji had run with the attitude. Why bother putting in any serious effort. We are 'so' far behind the main teams. The distance between my team, and the rest of the top teams is embarrassing, so I will just canter up the straight to the finish line. I would have understood, if she had run with that attitude.

Instead, while the Sun glistened on her body, I saw her using 'every' muscle and fibre in her arms and legs as she sprinted down that final straight, giving it - absolutely, everything! As if her team was, running for the gold medal! I hoped those nearby me, would not notice the tears of admiration, running down my cheeks.

Conclusion

It is the attitude of the three I have described, and others like them, that inspires admiration, and makes, most of us humble. The blind man, who did not consider his disability, a reason to stay at home, and so travelled about with confidence; using every one (apart from sight) of the sensory faculties that we all have.

The woman in Africa, who lives in the most

basic housing with just one change of clothing and a few personal possessions like a metal cooking pot, yet who is a person who is thankful to God - for all His blessings, and who considered it a privilege, to offer her visitor; hospitality.

The woman from Fiji, whose team was last by a country-mile but who sprinted down that final straight, giving it absolutely everything - all the way to the finish! A person who put in a, real gold medal performance!

60 Experiences That Humble

Chapter 7

Jesus-An Example of Humility

Paul wrote

> "Your attitude should be the same as that of Jesus Christ: Who, being in very nature God, did not consider equality with God something to be grasped, but made himself nothing, taking the very nature of a servant being made in human likeness.
>
> And being found in appearance as a man, he humbled himself and became obedient to death, even death on a cross!" Phil 2:5-8

There are three aspects to Jesus humility highlighted in these verses. The first was his willingness to shed the powers and glory of heaven, for human likeness. We humans, and particularly we who live today in developed countries with all the conveniences of modern societies; often take for granted all sorts of gadgets and machines and means of transportation and technological advances that people living a century ago, would have considered so advanced, as to be, unthinkable. It is easy from the perspective of what we have and what we can achieve with the aid of today's technology, to consider that we are the apex of life, in the universe.

While it is true we are the most advanced animal species, and have come so far, the heights we are at present and will progress to (provided we don't destroy ourselves in the meantime) are minimal compared to what Jesus was, and is now - and will become to the people of this earth

He came from heaven to share our humanity. He existed long before the universe, our galaxy and solar system came into being. He knew what it was like to be a central part of the glorious life of God's throne room (described by the Apostle John in Revelation chapter four). In heaven, he had at his command, about 72,000 angels. C.f. Matt 26:53

This Jesus, who had so much power and glory before coming to this Earth, offered hints during his ministry here on Earth; that he had come from another realm. A realm where he was used to thinking that, nothing is impossible. When Jesus began his ministry; he demonstrated that he was used to thinking, 'everything is possible. Examples of the way Jesus was used to thinking that, everything is impossible, include:

- He walked on water.
- He rebuked a storm, and the weather instantly became calm.
- He cursed a tree and it died.
- He knew where large shoals of fish were on Lake Galilee even though Peter (an experienced fisherman) had tried all night without success to find any.
- He multiplied five loaves and two fish (a boys' lunch) so that it would feed five thousand.
- At his word, sight was given to a blind person, people could hear again, the sick were cured; and lepers were instantly healed.

At one stage, he was with Moses and Elijah, and the three were transformed into a bright glory on a mountain, and then after his resurrection, appeared to two disciples on the road to Emmaus but as soon as they recognized him, disappeared and when he left the earth, ascended into the clouds, without any assistance.

Not only did he offer during his ministry, strong hints that he had come from another realm where anything and everything was possible. He knew that he would come again; a second time as. King of kings and Lord of Lords or as we might say today. He will come again as the President of Presidents, or the Prime Minister of Prime Ministers. Or the CEO, of all CEO's, and will be one before whom, 'every' knee will bow.

When he comes again, the second time. Every Olympic gold medallist. Every recipient of the Nobel Prize. Every film star. Every C.E.O. Every Supreme Court judge and every world leader of any sort; will all bow before him! And when they (and we) bow before him, I don't believe anyone will need to be commanded to bow before him, because of the booming voice of a large angel, standing over us.

Or feel obligated to do so, because that is an appropriate thing to do when we are in the presence of, the "King of kings" - the President of all time. Our bowing low before the "King of Kings", (or the President of all time), will simply be because we will see his unmatched power and glory, and every fibre of our being will sense that we truly are in the presence of the Son of God. Then we will bow as naturally as a flower bends before the wind. And when we bow low, we will feel it is both a privilege and an honour, to do so.

Both who Jesus was before coming to this Earth and who he will be when he returns; a second time; are background to what Paul wrote in his letter to the church at Philippi. Jesus voluntarily came to this Earth; as a servant leader. That servant leader nature was demonstrated supremely, before his crucifixion, when he washed the disciples feet.

By this stage, the disciples were usually calling him either "Lord" or "Master"; and if anything, they should have washed Jesus' feet for that task was normally done by the servants, of the house.

The way Jesus humbled himself to become a servant leader; is an example for us - to be, servant Christians. There is a sense in which we are precious and loved and important; because we are children of God who have been given a for-taste of heaven through the Holy Spirit living in us. At the same time, following both Jesus' words and example, we are truly Christians if we consider ourselves; servants of, a servant king.

Willing to do any task in the kingdom of God. Some of those tasks may be in the Church; others tasks may be; anywhere we go, and for whoever we meet - during the course of a normal day. Servants see themselves as people willing to: give, pray for or with, help, assist, encourage, speak to; any other person - for their good. Some of those tasks may be accomplished in a Church setting or within a Christian organisation, but most of the words spoken and actions undertaken by Christians; will never be published because we are servants of the king; and as servants, do not request or desire, recognition.

The second aspect of Jesus humility highlighted in Paul's leter to the church at Philippi, was Jesus' obedience, "even death on a cross!" Obeying God's will, is at the core of what it means to be Christian. To do God's will, not our own. That aspect of the Christian life is identified in the Lord's prayer. After the first lines of the Prayer ("Our Father in heaven, hallowed by your name, your kingdom come...."), are the words.

> *Your will be done on earth as it is in heaven*

That is what Jesus did, and that is what he wants us, his followers to do. To be people who will say, …

> "not as I will, but as you will." Matt 26:39

It takes humility to say to ourselves. Not my way, but your way. Not my will but, your will.

Chapter 6

Walking Humbly With God

In this chapter, I will be urging people to walk humbly with God.

Before expanding on that thought; have you considered the other side of the coin? That God, the creator of the universe; humbles himself to walk with us, talk with us, and love mere human beings; us! David hinted at God's great humility, when he penned these words.

> "When I look at the night sky and see the work of your fingers - the moon and the stars you set in place - what are mere mortals that you

> should think about them, human beings that you should care about them?" Psalm 8:3-4 NLT

We humans have a tendency to look at human achievements; and say "wow". We humans have created huge cities; and dams and space rockets and luxury liners and every four years, sporting extravaganzas like the Olympics which are held in large, colourful stadiums.

These large cities with their sky scrapers, and space rockets and huge cruise liners and people stacked stadiums; are a far cry from the day humans lived in wooden/earth homes, and were limited to sending arrows through the air and travel was by foot or horse or a basic boat. However, our greatest achievements; will always pale into insignificance; when compared with; the greatness, the glory the and majesty of God.

It always a good exercise for us busy Christians to wait for a night when there is a clear sky; and then walk outside - and be still for even five minutes; and while outside - try and take in the breath-taking expanse of space, and recognise that what we can only see with our eyes; is only the minutest fraction of the size of the universe.

Humility is not about denying ourselves, but simply acknowledging God for who he is.

Our God is bigger than the universe; yet humbles himself to care about, and talk to, and listen to; we – earthlings. The huge expanse of the universe and the greatness of God; naturally lead to the words of the prophet Micah.

> "..O people, the Lord has told you what is good,
> and this is what he requires of you:
> to do what is right, to love mercy,
> and to walk humbly with your God." Mic 6:8 (NLT)

The prophet Micah used the word 'walk'. We know that for any able-bodied person, walking is a natural, daily exercise. Usually we do not even think about the fact that we are walking – for when we want to get something in our home or place of work, we just get up, and walk! Because Micah used the word 'walk', we can take it that, being in daily contact with God our Father, is meant to be both a natural and a daily, occurrence. However Micah added the adjective, 'humbly' to the word, walk.

Why walk humbly with God? It is not a

question we would even ask, if we knew how great God is. How powerful, intelligent, loving, forgiving, understanding, holy, and perceptive, the eternal God is. The amazing fact is, a God of 'unlimited power', wants to have relationship with human beings like us who, require a fork-lift to lift anything much heavier than a suitcase.

The amazing fact is. A God of unlimited knowledge, wants to talk to beings like us. Beings who know less than one percent of the total information available to the human race. And the amount of information the most intelligent person on Earth knows; is decreasing as a percentage; every day.

It is amazing, that a God of unlimited love loves us - and every person on Earth, and is willing to receive - what little drops of love, we give in return. It is amazing that a God, who is not limited by time, has the time to listen to us, no matter who we are or where we are, or when we call.

A God who never needs food or sleep or any other form of sustenance, is willing to lead guide and talk to human beings, who need; lots of all three.

A God who, though knowing the names of

every star in the most distant galaxy, and also know our name and the names of every person on earth; and considers us, special.

> *If we even begin to understand who God is, we will naturally, walk humbly with Him.*

Ann Spangler wrote

> "When it comes to love and marriage, the strangest match of all history is the one between God and his people. At first glance it looks like a complete mismatch! A holy God linked to weak and sinful human beings. Greatness linked to smallness. Wisdom linked to folly. Yet God says: "I will betroth you forever."

Guidance is linked to being humble. One of the benefits of being humble, is that when God see's we are humble enough to consider doing things His way, He guides us. David wrote.

> *"He guides the humble in what is right and teaches them his way."*
> *Psa 25:9*

I suggest that when God sees humility in a person's heart, He says to himself. 'This is a person I can speak to and guide. When planning the birth of his Son; God looked around Israel for a woman with a humble heart. It is implicit in the Gospels, that when he saw that quality in Mary, the future mother of Jesus, he decided to send the angel Gabriel to ask her, to be the mother of Jesus. Her response was

> "I am the Lord's servant. May it be
> to me as you have said." Luke 1:38
> (N.I.V)

When Mary used the word "servant". She did not mean, she was of a servant status, but like a servant; she was willing to do what God, asked her to do. God had seen that willingness in her heart; and therefore decided to approach her about fulfilling his purposes. It was the humble willingness of Mary that pleased God, and God must have said to Himself.

"I can do business with, her. She can be fulfilled by doing my will and I will bless her and others will appreciate what she has done, in my name."

Later, Mary went to visit her cousin Elizabeth. While staying with her cousin, she spoke a prayer of praise. In that prayer of praise, Mary recognised that God "scatters the proud", and exalts the humble.

In an ideal, we would be continually humble, but for all of us, pride can creep in. However, that is not the end of the story. We can still turn to God; and humble ourselves; if we are in trouble; or even if we are not in trouble. Two common words in the Bible are "turn to the Lord" and equally, "return to the Lord."

The Apostle Peter wrote about those times when things begin to go seriously wrong, and we begin to call upon Him.

> *"Humble yourselves, therefore, under God's mighty hand, that he may lift you up in due time. Cast all your anxiety on him because he cares for you." 1 Pet 5:6&7*

NB There is a similar verse in 2 chronicles 7:14.

The reasons Peter recommends we humble ourselves before God and cast our cares on him, are four-fold. He was confident that:

- God 'knows' about our problems/difficulties.
- God 'cares' about us.
- God is 'able' to lift us up.
- God is able to take care of 'all' (every/any) burden.

For most Christians, life is a journey with, all sorts of challenges, twists and turns, and God will lift our burdens – if we humble ourselves and share them with him, and in faith ask for his help.

Chapter 7

Pride

It was inevitable in a book about humility, that a chapter about pride, is included. The word 'proud' (which obviously describes a person with pride), appears 48 times in the King James Bible. The word 'proudly' appears 10 times in that Bible. The word 'proudly' is translated in the more modern N.I.V version of the Bible into words like; *arrogantly, arrogant* and *arrogance*. In one instance it is translated as 'boast'.

Even though the words are different in the newer versions, we get the same idea that the old fashioned word 'proudly', conveys. That a prideful person is someone who will boast, or be arrogant, or act arrogantly.

It is interesting that the word 'proud' and its derivatives (like arrogantly, arrogant and arrogance) are five times more common in the Bible, than the words 'humility' and 'humble'. The Bible can be like that at times, more commonly pointing out what it is against, than what it is for. Bur each time it tells you what it is against, it is also really telling you what it is for – in this case, humility.

What is noticeable about the use of the word *pride* in the Bible and its close associates like *arrogance, arrogantly* and *arrogant*; is that the verses containing those words, can be classified into four categories:

1   Those that tell us that pride and arrogance – affects our relationship with God.
2   Those that tell us God is against pride and arrogance – because it harms other people.
3   Those that tell of the about harm to other people, caused by pride and arrogance.
4   Those that tell of the harm to our self, caused by pride and arrogance.

Before looking at different types of pride in people, lets' look at it form a divine perspective. Satan, a being (a Son?) God created, is no longer in heaven and is now opposed to anything God does; because Satan became; proud. Pride is something, Satan and his minions, encourage and applauds in human beings; in the same way that s the Father/ Son and Holy Spirit; encourage and applaud humility. Solomon in the book of Proverbs wrote:

> "I hate pride and arrogance, evil behaviour and perverse speech." Prov 8:13b (N.I.V)

From a divine perspective; pride and arrogance are not merely something that the Father/Son and Holy Spirit; dislike. They hate pride and I suggest the reason they hate it is, because they know the harm pride does to an individual, to groups and to nations; and the harm it causes to other; individuals, groups or nations.

Tests of pride

In an earlier chapter about humility, I wrote a list of characteristics of, humble people. It is appropriate to repeat that list here, except the heading has been be changed to – proud people do not.

Proud people do not like:

- Admitting they make mistakes
- Admitting they have faults

- Admitting they are sinners (and will continue to sin and fall short of God's perfect standards, till the day we die)
- Admitting to themselves they are wrong
- Admitting to others they are wrong
- Admitting they have a problem
- Admitting someone in their family has a problem
- Admitting they don't know the answer to a particular problem
- Admitting they do not know the answer to a question about the faith
- Admitting that they sometimes, get guidance wrong
- Being led by others
- Receiving advice from others
- Receiving praise, thanks and compliments from others
- Do not like receiving gifts,
- Do not like receiving gifts of money, or help from others
- Will not readily dismiss any mistakes they have made
- Do not like being corrected

This list is not exhaustive and is not meant to be, guilt producing; but maybe that list is a gentle reminder that we, all have pride of some sort - in some measure.

How do we know if we have pride? As I thought about the subject; I came to realise that I can tell (or at least can detect more easily than before) when I have put on the clothing of pride. (There is the clothing of humility; and also the clothing of pride)

When I have put on the clothing of pride, there is a note of derision in my voice about someone else's opinion who I, disagree with. Or I catch myself, putting someone down or I have a feeling of superiority.

The second way to detect pride is to 'listen' to what others are saying to us or about us. They may be saying something like. "You do not listen to my opinion." Or, "When I do that, you hit the roof, but when you do the same thing, you justify your actions." If we are not listening to others or criticising others for doing something while at the same time justifying ourselves doing the same thing; the root cause is likely to be pride.

The third way to detect pride, is to pray a prayer, something like this.

"Lord, I'm not aware of any pride in me, but maybe it is there and I am not aware of it. Please show me, in your time and in your own way. Amen

NB Usually the Holy Spirit is very gentle and patient, and will pick the right time to let us know.

Four observations about pride_

The first observation is that there is something very significant about the spelling of the word pride, which provides a hint of how it becomes resident in a person's life. That is, the letter 'i' is in the middle of the word. I am sure that in most instances of pride, it is the 'i' factor, that is the cause of pride.

Second, there is something else about pride. Pride is something that 'creeps' into our thinking and values, rather than being something we set out to learn about, or seek to buy. Few people who are proud, set out to become proud. Probably no proud person ever said to themselves. "One of my goals in life, is to become proud!"

Pride is not like that. It is not something we learn about or can buy. It is just something that 'creeps' into our attitudes and thinking - usually unnoticed! It often creeps in when we accumulate, 'more' of something. When we accumulate 'more' goods, or 'more' knowledge, or 'more' power – and once we are on that journey to gaining more and accumulating more, we begin to compare ourselves with others.

In the Living Bible, it says Uzziah, '*became*' proud. 2 Chron 26:16 (Italics added)

> "He wasn't proud at birth or at the start of his reign. He became proud during his reign as king."

Pride, crept in.

Thirdly, many who are proud, do not consider themselves proud, because pride has a habit of disguising it's presence when it creeps into our thought-life and attitudes, and it is only when our pride is pricked, that it is apparent that it is there. In most cases; people who are proud, do not consider they are proud, and will justify their thoughts, words and actions.

And the fourth observation: I would rather not write this paragraph and would be happy to write, that we can conquer pride; 'once and for all', however I don't believe that is the case. We may have been humble yesterday or last week or last year, but that does mean we will be humble today, for pride can creep back in again, even in small doses.

The Pharaoh at the time of Moses was like that. He was stubbornly proud through all the various plagues and calamities. Then when the last plague came upon the Egyptians, he was momentarily, humble, asking Moses to pray for him. But once the Hebrew people had gone, he became proud again and decided that an itinerant shepherd called Moses, was not going to escape with his, prized slaves.

I was surprised to read in a book by written by Yonghi Cho, senior pastor of the world's largest (single) church, wrote that 'daily' he confessed his sins and asked God to keep him from lust and pride. Surely, one would think, that the leader of the world's largest (single) Church, had got to a state that the rest of us Christians can only dream about. A state of no longer having any sins or faults like lust and pride.

That humble acknowledgement by Pastor Yonghi Cho, is an acknowledgement that our humility of yesterday, will not necessarily carry on over, to today.

Examples of the 'I' factor

Several people from the Bible, illustrate how the 'I' factor, can be an indication that pride has taken hold.

In the book of Daniel, there is an account of King Nebuchadnezzar of Babylon walking on the roof of the royal palace (I'm sure it would have been the largest building in the city) and saying to himself.

> "Is not this the great Babylon I have built as my royal residence, by my mighty power and for the glory of my majesty?" Dan 4:30 (N.I.V)

Excavations of the city of Babylon show that 90% of the bricks used to construct the buildings in the city of Babylon, have king Nebuchadnezzar's initials, printed on them. So it was no idle boast of King Nebuchadnezzar when he spoke those words, "Is not this the great Babylon I have built as my royal residence, by my mighty power and for the glory of my majesty?

It was immediately after king Nebuchadnezzar had spoken those words, that he became insane, and was driven out of the palace and lived much like an animal until he acknowledged that it was God who had allowed him to rule in the first place.

There are four significant words in that short sentence he spoke, while walking on his palace roof. They are, "I", "my", "my" and "my" His thinking revolved around 'his' achievements. ...I have built..... my royal residence.... my mighty power ....my majesty? Once Nebuchadnezzar humbled himself and acknowledged it was God who allows rulers to rule, his sanity was restored and he was restored to his throne, the Bible records his new way of thinking and acting. For he said, "Now I" – "praise and exalt, and glorify the King of heaven," He also acknowledged his royal advisors.

I am sure the same process happens today, when people become powerful. 'Some' begin to get awed by their achievements and power and status, and pride creeps in, in various ways. Politicians for example, may speak at a venue about the value of families and family values in the hope of winning votes or maintaining their support; all the while cheating on their wives or partners; or visiting prostitutes.

For some, their pride about their high status, leads them to feel they are above the law and do not need to declare their full earnings to the Inland Revenue Service, or that. Because of their high status in society, they can use their power to their own advantage – all the while condemning others who may do like-wise.

Another example from the Bible where the "I" factor was significant in a person's pride, comes from a story Jesus told about two men who went up to the Temple to pray. One was a tax collector, and the other a Pharisee. It is said that the Pharisee prayed.

> "God, I thank you that I am not like other men – robbers, evil doers, adulterers – or even like this tax collector. I fast twice a week and give a tenth of all I get." Luke 18:11-12

The word "I" is found four times in that short prayer, a prayer that was really a monologue commending his own goodness to God and others, and making comparisons with obviously sinful people like; robbers, evil doers, adulterers and tax collectors. People he believed to be at the opposite end of the scale of God's approval, to himself.

Jesus compared that prayer of the Pharisee with the prayer of the tax collector who beat his chest about his unworthiness. Jesus' final words were.

> "For everyone who exalts himself will be humbled, and he who humbles himself will be exalted." Luke 18:14

The example of the proud Pharisee, suggests that 'pride and judgementalism' are linked, just as 'humility and mercy', are linked. We can see the link between humility and mercy on an occasion when the teachers of the law bought to Jesus a woman caught in the act of adultery, an act they pointed out deserved stoning. Jesus tried to get them to show mercy to her by saying

> "He who is without sin, may cast the first stone."

In saying those words, Jesus was trying to get the Pharisees to be honest with themselves and admit they were sinners too. They may not have sinned in the same way as this woman caught in adultery, but may have lied or sinned in some other; not so obvious way.

There is a saying,

> "there but for the grace of God go I",

That saying picks up the principle contained in Jesus statement to the Pharisees.

It is easy for modern-day Christians, to slip into a mindset of Pharisee-bashing, and think. 'I don't stand on corners and pray prayers like the proud Pharisees', but I suspect there is a bit of the Pharisee in all of us, that likes to think we are better than others. Nebuchadnezzar's pride was a result of his great wealth, power and achievements. The

Pharisee's pride was a result of their spiritual achievements like regular prayer and fasting. Their moral life-style and their great knowledge of the Old Testament; and all its laws – compared to say, the sinful tax collector.

A great example of a humble approach to others sinfulness, is contained in this quote from Bill Hybels, found in his book, *Just Walk Across The Room*. The context of the quote was that he was talking to a tearful man who had just paid for a woman to have an abortion.

> *"I didn't skim over the seriousness of what he had done, but I was extremely careful not to torment him any further by rubbing his face in his sin. Every time I'm confronted with the depravity of someone else's sin, all I can think about is my own fallen state and my proneness to fall short of God's standard."* p91 (Zondervan)

Contemporary examples of the 'I' factor

Position and power can be a dangerous cocktail when they combine. That was true in the past and sadly, is still true today. When (some) people today rise to positions of power and importance, pride often creeps in, and they begin acting as if they are above the law, or do not have to observe the normal moral boundaries. The latest announcement that (and examples like this occur regularly across a spectrum of democratic countries) a powerful public figure has been having regular affairs or regularly visits prostitutes or has abused his or her power in some way; is so common, that it does not surprise most people today.

Even if the expose is not about them cheating on their partner, or the regular use of prostitutes; it may that the person who became enthralled by their elevated status; did not disclose all the relevant information on their tax return. Or in some other way, they have mis-used the power of their office.

The prophet Jeremiah spoke of a deceitful heart (Jer 17:9), and it seems that, 'if' pride creeps into a person's heart, they can publically espouse integrity in Government or publically espouse family values (if that will help them win votes), while cheating behind their partners back or misusing their position of power for personal gain.

Deceit appears to compartmentalise a person.

In one compartment, can be found, what they 'know' is right and tell others is right – while in another compartment can be found, their real thoughts and actions which, because they are sealed off from the right and wrong compartment by deceit; allows them the freedom to act in a way they know is wrong and yet tell others, that such actions, are wrong.

Deceit helps keeps our actions, and what we know is right; in separate rooms. Because deceit has taken hold, the response of many is, not. "I was wrong", rather. "It was an error of judgement!" Often there is a half-attempt to bridge the gap between the two compartments, resulting in a half apology, because deceit still holds a strong, influence. And if they can make a villian out of the person or persons who exposed them, all the better. It helps shift the blame.

Before we throw too many brick-bats at secular, political and public figures; we Christians have to admit to our own, hall of shame. Stories of Christian leaders who have sexually abused children or Christian leaders who have become involved in the same sort of activities described above, sadly happen with some frequency. The reason these 'hall of shame' actions happen, is relevant to this chapter. Billy Graham wrote in his book called *The Journey.*

> *A friend of mine who is a seminary professor once listed the Christian leaders who he knew who had fallen into sexual sin. Almost without exception, he said, the real cause was pride.*

That surprised me, that is; the reason for the fall. If the seminary professor had written that among the reasons for Christian leaders falling into sexual sin, were those below, I would have understood.

1 *The work-load of the Christian leader was too great, and not having enough quality time with his or her partner, the Christian leader had an affair.*
2 *The leader was away from home too often on speaking engagements, and that factor eventually led them to giving in to the temptation of using a prostitute.*
3 *They became addicted to internet pornography, despite preaching about the temptation of internet pornography, and that led to.....*

However, the reason for the fall into sexual sin given by the seminary professor, was none of these obvious reasons, but – pride! I do not know any of the individuals the seminary professor was referring to, or any of the circumstances, so I cannot make any comment, with any sort of credibility about their individual cases. But let's review the possible reasons that I gave above; and consider how, *pride* might have been the *ultimate* reason, for the fall into sexual sin.

1:   The work-load of the leader was so great that they did not have time to spend with their marriage partner.

Was it pride that dictated the amount of work the Christian leader took on board, rather than admit they could only cope with so much work, and needed help to accomplish the work load? Remember in an earlier chapter I admitted I had three crashes in a company vehicle, over a short period to time. At that stage I was 'proud' about my go – go - go life-style, and how much I could achieve in any given day.

2:   The Christian leader was away-from-home frequently on speaking engagements, and eventually they gave in to the readily available the services of a prostitute?

Was it pride that drove the Christian leader to

accept, so many (too many) speaking engagements away-from-home rather than; following the leading of the Holy Spirit and limiting the number of engagements.

3:　　　***They became addicted to internet pornography, despite preaching about the temptation of internet pornography, and that led to.....***

Was is it the pride in the leader that said. I can look at pornographic material and not be affected by it, even though ordinary Christians should not be doing this and they will become addicted to the lure of pornographic images? But not I.

Possibly the same sort of pride that seems to be at work in public figures who speak of family values and yet who use prostitutes/have affairs; is at work in some Christian leaders as well. In the case of the Christian leader, the thinking might be. 'It is important for members of my congregation or those who I speak to at conferences, to recognise that sinful actions, lead to harm. But being a leader: I am 'above' having to recognise the consequences of sin'. Such can be, the deceitfulness of a heart that has, pride in it.

"Lord, please forgive me for my pride. Spirit of truth, please reveal any hidden pride that I am not aware of. Amen."

Chapter 8

Different Forms of Pride

There are different forms of pride and only some will be detailed, in this chapter. Two have already been mentioned in the previous chapter. One is the pride that (may) come from having power, position and wealth; such as King Nebuchadnezzar had. The second type of pride was the type the Pharisees had, who had become very proud about their holy and righteous living, and about their knowledge of the law – compared to others who they regarded as, sinners.

Other forms of pride touched on in this book, could be called relational or personal pride, which will be expanded on, later in this chapter. As I reflected on the nature of pride in its various guises, it occurred to me that there are some natural partners to pride - though I need to add. These partners do not always go together. For example, in the Bible; men like Joseph, David and Daniel had power, but no obvious pride.

The natural partners

- Power and pride
- Pride and prejudice
- Pride and blindness (particularly to one's own faults)
- Pride and dogmatic self reliance
- Pride and dogmatism
- Pride and racial superiority
- Scriptural error, and pride

Racial pride

A pastor asked his congregation, "can racism be justified by the Bible?" After about a thirty second pause, his answer was. "Not if we look at the beginning of the Bible, or the end of the Bible or anywhere in between?" Unfortunately I did not write down the Bible references he quoted at the time to back up that statement, but from memory; they included some of these.

- "Be fruitful and increase in number; fill the earth...Gen 1:28

- "And I, because of their actions and imaginations, am about to come and gather all nations and tongues, and they will come and see my glory." Isa 66:18

- But the angel said to them, "Do not be afraid. I bring you good news and great joy that will be for all the people. Luke 2:10

- He said to them, "Go into all the world and preach the good news to all creation." Mark 16:15

- After this I looked and there before me was a great multitude that no one could count, from every tribe, people and language, standing before the throne and in front of the Lamb. Rev 7:9

Notice the inclusive language used in the verses above. "all nations", "all people", "all creation", and "every tribe, people and language."

Apart from those verses; it is noticeable that Jesus worked on the first disciples, to break down, their racial pride. The most despised race to Jews, were the Samaritans – a half breed. Jesus addressed that issue by talking to Samaritans, and by making a Samaritan, the 'hero' of a parable he told.

After Jesus returned to heaven, Jesus began to work on the prejudice of his Jewish disciples against foreigners. That process began when Peter was given a vision of unclean animals, and three times Peter was told to eat them. In the end the Lord Jesus told him that what God had called kosher, he was not to consider unclean.

Virtually straight away after the vision, a Roman soldier and two servants of a Centurion came calling for him. Peter admitted to the Centurion that he had been taught not to dine with foreigners. Later when Peter was at the house of the godly centurion Cornelius, the Holy Spirit fell on the "gentiles too", confirming the vision, that God has, no favourites, among the races.

Pride about our knowledge of the future

As I write this paragraph, I am looking at a newspaper cutting about a meeting of angry shareholders. Angry because, the returns promised on their investment in a scheme that traded in a raw material; had made significant losses. The promoters of the scheme, blamed a 'once in a life-time' weather pattern and the banking troubles of 2008, for the result.

At first glance, all the blame for the losses should be put on the shoulders of those who promoted the scheme, but that is a shallow way of looking at the problem. The reason those investors were angry (if they were really honest with themselves), is that first of all, there was an element of greed in their investment. If these investors were really honest with themselves, they would admit that they were trying to get a higher rate of return than what was available, through registered banks.

Secondly, if they were really honest; there is no such thing, as a 'fail-safe' investment. In financial history, many investments that have 'looked' sound, before investors have poured money into them; have come undone; for a variety of reasons. Reasons that became obvious; once the investment began to turn, sour.

The Bible touches on another aspect that investors and all who base their plans on the future; should take into account. Few people in the past one hundred years have predicted the calamities that have occurred.

> WW1,
> The great depression of the 1930's,
> WW11

> The oil crisis of 1971,
> The 1987 share market crash,
> Or the banking crisis of 2008/9.

To a large extent these calamities were caused by racial pride or the pride of greed.

The Bible is a very honest book at times and in it's pages we find words, like these.

> "Look here, you who say, "Today or tomorrow we are going to a certain town and will stay there a year. We will do business there and make a profit. How do you know what your life will be like tomorrow?....What you ought to say is, "If the Lord wants us to, we will live and do this or that." Otherwise you are boasting about your own plans....James 4:13-16 (abbrev) NLT

In business and in life it is necessary to make plans, to be successful but the point James was making. Few forsee such calamities and even fewer listen to those who predict them, so it is necessary to be humble enough to allow for the fact that, none of us, can be totally certain of the future. That is where faith comes in. We trust God that he knows about the future; whatever it may bring.

Some financial analysts are 'proud' they have

predicted the future financial course of a company and a country. While their analysis may be accurate from the information they have available; they and most others; cannot predict events that may occur because someone has acted out of racial, religious or economic pride. E.g. A 9/11 event or a Ponzi scheme.

A pride of 'knowing the future', is also characteristic of Christian sects and cults. They are proud that they can say. We know, *what where and when* this will occur. By contrast, humble faith says.

> *I may be able to tell the colours of the season but I do not know exactly when and how. I leave will that to God, and trust that He has, the timing in his hands.*

Pride can creep into so many areas of life; often on the back of good desires. I admitted in an earlier chapter that I had become a person who was committed to, ...making the most of every opportunity (my time), because the days are evil .... Eph 5:16 N.I.V That was a good desire, backed up by Scripture.

However, pride crept in on the back of that 'good' Scriptural desire; and I began to become proud of the way I maximised my time each day; compared to say others.

Some who, like me have become proud of their work output, have found their health, or their relationships, have suffered as a consequence.

Some readers may be saying. I do not have, fail-safe investments and I do not push myself; to achieve the absolute maximum; each day. Those two examples, were only included to reiterate the point that pride can creep into virtually every area of life. And when it does, it causes harm.

Pride and our relationships with other people

Pride damages all relationships we have, while humility heals and strengthens, all relationships we have. One way pride manifests itself in relationships; is in a. 'I am always right, attitude'. If we clothe ourselves with humility, then we will treat our opinion and the opinion of others; as of equal value. Like being on, a level plain. Once on that level plain, we will recognise that sometimes we will be right and other times wrong.

Pride entangles itself in many disagreements between people, making those disagreements, much harder to resolve, while humility dissolves most of the reasons for those disagreements. Rob Parsons wrote in his book *Loving Against The Odds.* "When we deny ourselves the luxury of having to win every argument, one of the products is that we avoid having arguments over details that don't really matter."

Intellectual pride

Paul wrote

> "Knowledge puffs up, but love builds up." I Cor 8:1 (N.I.V)

That can be true in both the religious world, and the secular world. I get the impression from what I read in the newspaper and in scientific magazines, that some almost *worship,* our ever increasing knowledge.

> *It is as if it is, their god, and the world's saviour.*

The impression gained is. 'Knowledge' is the world's answer to anything and everything. That notion is held, despite the obvious evidence that it is not – at least where human relationships are concerned. Instances of family members fighting against family members, neighbours against neighbours, employers against employees, investors against those they invested with, country against country e.t.a. show that despite our increasing knowledge and technological advances, the fundamental problems of human selfishness, jealousy and greed; remain. Problems that beset the human heart, soul, mind and spirit, which the Bible and Jesus in particular; tried/try, to address.

A pride about intellectual knowledge can creep into secular organisations; but also the Church. Satan, is the master of disguise; has not gone away or gone to sleep. He has plans for the Church today; and though he is a defeated foe, has plans and schemes (Eph 6:11) for the Church. I once read a quote that gelled.

> *Satan can work through both great wealth, and great poverty. Satan can work through great ignorance, and great education.*

Great education; can also be a vehicle of pride. Paul identified one way that intellectual pride, can work against accepting, spiritual truth. In his view, it prevented people hearing the Gospel message. He wrote

> "Jews demand miraculous signs
> and Greeks look for wisdom, but

> we preach Christ crucified: a stumbling block to Jews, and foolishness to Gentiles....For the foolishness of God is wiser than mans wisdom, 1 Cor 1:22-25 (abbrev N.I.V.)

The Gospel message is admittedly, foolish to those with intellectual pride, for our minds find it hard to fathom and reason how the death of Jesus on a cross outside of Jerusalem nearly two thousand years ago, could mean. Complete forgiveness of every sin we confess, and reconciliation with God.

Pride in their knowledge, is what maintains Christian sects. At first glance, meeting people from Christian sects like Jehovah's Witnesses and Mormons, tells you that these are humble people – and in many areas and in many ways – they are. But dig a little deeper and get in a lengthy conversation with them, and their pride becomes apparent. Their pride in 'knowing the truth', and how to interpret the Bible. Their belief that their church is truly, 'the only true Church'. Or their belief that, 'only' people from 'their' flock will get to heaven in the case of Mormons, or in the case of Jehovah's Witnesses. Only 'they' will be leaders in the thousand year reign on earth.

I have seen pride in the Liberal theological movement, that came into force last century. I trained at a liberal theological college, for three years. And people I can recall, were so , 'proud' about the way they have questioned, all the traditional beliefs of Christianity, and the accuracy of the Bible.

Some have become so proud about the way they have questioned the traditional beliefs of the faith, that they will not question their new found faith of 'unbelief'. For example, I have told people who consider that the Bible has myths and legends in it, that I have a computer disc full of evidence solid archaeological evidence that the Bible is true, and they show no interest.

That suggests to me they are people who have became so proud of their (so called) open-minded questioning of the accuracy of the Bible, that they have, closed their minds to the possibility that every major phase and person mentioned in the Bible, can be supported by archaeology. Their new-found faith of 'questioning the accuracy of the Bible' – has come with a dose of pride – and that pride has closed their minds to any evidence that questions, their new found faith.

The proud, readily maintain error.

It is easy to throw brick-bats at Liberal Christians but in my opinion; other theological streams in the Church can also ingest pride. Pride can creep into 'solid Evangelical Bible colleges'. For example, in some, there appears to be a great relish in using various methodologies, to analyse, the content of the Bible. Or using what I call. 'Scholarly Evangelical terminology' that the average Christian does not use, and cannot understand.

Other examples include a focus on schematic explanations on how the Gospels and Bible came into existence – as if that really mattered. Or schematic explanations of why the events of the book of Revelation have, 'already' occurred.

The Charismatic/Pentecostal stream is no different. People can be affected by pride in that stream too. It seems to me that some of the leaders in this stream of the Church, have become proud of the rapid growth of their churches, so that all they want to talk about is; not Jesus teachings, but. 'Personal success' and 'church growth'.

Personal success and church growth have

effectively become their new religion instead of ensuring that each person contacted by their church is challenged to become an effective disciple of Jesus – and after that. Making an effort to ensure they, stay an effective disciple of Jesus.

There has been a brief attempt during the last pages, to show that, all theological branches of the Church, are vulnerable, to pride.

Pride in our Church

There are different forms of 'Church' pride. One is a pride about our theological stream. It might be semi-Liberal, or Conservative or Evangelical or Pentecostal. We can also become proud about our local Church. Usually having a healthy pride in our local Church, is a good thing, but it is possible to slide from having a healthy pride in our local Church, to go on from there - to having a pride that suggests, ours is, 'the Church'.

People listening to Christians who have an unhealthy pride in their church, manifest that pride by an attitude – ours is 'the Church' – and they give the 'impression' that. If Jesus were to come to their county or town or city today; he would by-pass, all the other nearby churches, and make a bee-line, straight for, 'their' Church!

I have found myself talking like that, about the Church I am attending.

Then there is the pride of being 'Catholic' or 'Protestant'. Let's pretend for a moment, I am *a proud Protestant*. Proud of the way our tradition challenged the abuses and theological errors in the Catholic Church; and brought the Church; back to the Bible. In the (*imaginary .i.e. It never took place but is told like a parable, to make a point*) scenario that follows, I meet a Catholic Christian. After a few moments of conversation, this Catholic proudly tells me.

C: "I belong to the true Church. Our Popes, go all the way back to St Peter."

Knowing a bit about history, I take the opportunity to prick his bubble, and tell him.

P: "Did you know that at one stage, there were three Popes?" After a short pause. "From what I can tell, that situation had nothing to do with God. Rather, just power politics." Then, in order to drive the dagger in further, I describe some of the immoral actions of some of the Popes and end by saying. St Peter would have turned in his grave, if he had seen some of the immoral and ruthless activities of, some of those popes"

Then having satisfied myself that I have done a good job at destroying this Catholics belief, that his Church is "the true Church", based on the lineage back to St Peter, I being a proud Protestant, am not finished. Before we part, I raised a question about the teachings, of his Church.

P: " Why do you pray to Mary. In the Bible there is only one mediator between God and the human race – and that mediator; is Jesus.

C: "Well that is our tradition."

P: "Tradition. " The true Church, bases its teachings and practices on the Bible. Not tradition!"

After a while this conversation has become so uncomfortable for the Catholic, the Catholic person, moves on. After they have gone; I, *the proud Protestant,* am satisfied that I have made the point about what defines, what is, the *true* Church. The true Church bases its teachings and practices on the Bible; and not tradition.

About short while later, I meet a being called 'Truth'. Truth seems to be some sort of heavenly being (maybe an angel in disguise) so I am glad to strike up a conversation. It does not take long before I tell Truth that I am a Christian from a "Bible-teaching, Bible-practicing, Church" and the conversation flows, from there.

Myself: "I'm pleased to meet you Truth. You are the type of person who will be impressed that I worship in a Church that teaches and practices the truths of the Bible." Truth's reply, greatly surprised me.

Truth: "It is interesting you say that you belong to a church that "that teaches and practices the truths of the Bible", it is my observation, that most churches are somewhat selective about what they teach and practice, from the Bible."

Myself: (Responding quickly). "That may be true of 'some' churches (and I was thinking of the Catholic tradition and a few other churches), where tradition plays a role in defining what they teach and practice, but in 'our' Church, we only teach and practice, what is in the Bible!

Truth looked at me as if questioning what I had just said then after a pause, asked. "Does your church have a Bishop?"

Myself: "Well no. We don't have Bishops (and

thinking of the Bishops I had seen in long robes), I asked. Isn't that a position that arose out of tradition, in some churches?"

Truth: "No. The word Bishop is mentioned six times in four New Testament books. (1&2 Tim, Titus and 2 Peter)"

Myself: "Well, ... apart from that one oversight, we practice what the Bible teaches."

Truth: "Interesting" said Truth. "How often do you take Holy Communion?"

Myself: "It is our tradition, to take it, every four weeks." NB As soon as I spoke the word "tradition", I regretted it. Because that is exactly what I had accused the Catholic Christian of - being part of a church who practices were based on tradition – but standing in front of Truth, I could not think of a better word.

Truth: "In your tradition" Truth queried? "Does your Church base it practices on tradition, rather than the Bible?"

Truth continued: "Jesus said, "As often as you meet, do this to remember me."

Myself: "Well..... apart from the two exceptions you have raised, we teach and practice what the Bible teaches."

Truth: "Is it possible that there are other teachings of the Bible, your Church does not practice?"

Myself: Now, and being, a little bit more humble, I begin to rack my brain in case Truth identified, any more examples of ways our Church; did not follow, Bible teachings, so I said. "Well, I can't think of any more examples of ways we do not practice what the Bible teaches."

Truth: "Tell me. Do you confess your sins, in Church, each Sunday?"

Myself: (Now on the defensive). "No, confessing sins is a tradition they have in some churches, where they have a liturgy. But we believe tradition kills the spirit of worship, so we do not have a liturgical type of service, in which we confess our sins."

Truth: "But I thought you said, your Church, teaches and practices, what is in the Bible?"

Myself: "Well, we do, but there are a few exceptions, like those you have raised."

Truth asks: "Do you read your Bible?"

Myself. "Of course!"

Truth. "Do you study it?"

Myself. "Yes we Protestants make a point of knowing what it teaches."

Truth "If you knew what the Bible teaches, you would confess your sins each Sunday; or at least in private - at home. "

Myself: Now on the defensive, I ask. "Where does it teach that we should confess our sins? What verses, are you referring to?"

Truth: "First of all Jesus said. "If anyone one of you is without sin, he may cast the first stone." John 8:7 (N.I.V) Then Truth added. "In the Lord's prayer, Jesus also taught the disciples to pray. "Forgive us our debts/wrongs/sins (depending on the translation). Matt 6:12 Jesus used the words, "our". He was not referring to those committed prior to your becoming a Christian; but the ones, committed since becoming a Christian. So the Son of God taught that God's people (disciples of Jesus) commit sins, and need to ask forgiveness for them."

Truth continued. Then there is the writings of the Apostle Paul. He wrote, …

> "for all have sinned, and fall short
> of the glory of God." Rom 3:23
> (N.I.V)

Those words are present tense and include 'all' people. The Apostle Paul also wrote later in his life, "I am the chief of sinners."

And the Apostle John wrote

> "If we claim to be without sin, we deceive ourselves and the truth is not in us." 1 John 1:7 (N.I.V)

John wrote those words, later in his life after a very long and godly life; yet he used the inclusive word, "we". So he was including himself when he wrote, "If we claim to be without sin, we deceive ourselves and the truth is not in us."

So to summarize. You have Jesus, the Son of God, saying that we all sin and key Apostles like Paul and John; also writing the same thing, so I come back to my earlier question. If your Church bases it's practices on the Bible, why do you not confess your sins in Church each Sunday; or at a minimum. Confess them at home?"

Myself. I was about to say, "we do not confess our sins in Church each Sunday; because it is not our tradition" but I knew I had already told that we base our teachings and practices on

the Bible and that Truth would pick me up -

straight away, if I used the word (tradition).

Then I began to look sheepish. I had accused the Catholic Christian of belonging to a Church that based it's practices on tradition – not the Bible - while ' Truth' had pointed out three examples of ways in which our Church; did not practice what is taught in the Bible – and the Catholic Church, did.

Soon I begin to indicate to indicate to Truth that, I must be going....

The intention of that imaginary scenario, was not to do a 'beat up', on any branch of the Church; Catholic or Protestant, or what ever. It was written to make the point, much like a parable. If pride has crept, we can begin to think that we belong to the 'true church' and take pride in that fact – because we have in pride concluded that ours is, the true church, it is likely we will think. 'Our Church teaches and practices, all that is in the Bible.

But if we were/are, even a little bit humble, we might acknowledge that there are some teachings and practices in our church (like others), that fall short of the ideal. As Truth had told me. Most churches are "selective" about what they teach and practice, from the Bible.

Listing various forms of pride can be discouraging. We may think we qualify for some, but then again, we may not be sure. One of the goals we have as Christians, is to live and walk humbly with God – with as little pride as possible, but that is not easy, when pride so easily, creeps in. Usually unnoticed.

However, unlike the other religions, we are not left alone - to our devices. Jesus said we have a "helper", called the Holy Spirit and, because he is the Spirit of truth, he will guide us if there are areas of our life, where there is hidden pride. All we need to do is pray a prayer like David prayed.

> *Examine me and test me, Lord; judge my desires and thoughts. Ps 26:2*

Follow up prayers might be. To confess the sin of pride that the Holy Spirit has brought to my/your attention. Then as a final act. Take that pride, and symbolically; leave it at the foot of the cross.

We are also privileged to have a faith which puts a strong emphasis, on grace. A grace given freely. A grace that helps us to admit our faults and recognise our errors, not so that we may be -left on the outer. Rather that we, like

Peter who denied Jesus three times; may get up again and walk, confident of his, unfailing and gracious love.

Loving ourself and pride

Pride is *out*, yet loving ourselves is *in* - according to the Bible. So how do we distinguish between the two? Jesus said, "You shall love your neighbour as you love yourself" but how do we distinguish between loving our self and pride? Let's start with two quotes that go a long way to distinguish between the two. A quote of Joyce Meyers is very helpful to distinguish between the two states. She said,

> *"We should love ourselves, but I don't mean we should be in love with ourselves."*

One of my quotes is

> *'Christianity is bad for one's pride, but good for one's self esteem'*

As a Christian, you and I are to consider ourselves, children of God. People who He knew about, even before we were born. People who Jesus died for. In a few words. People of eternal significance and worth! Notice I haven't mentioned looks or income or position or race or any other criteria that people may assess us by, to determine our value. We take our value from the one who has existed for all time.

Good pride

I can't think of any verse in the Bible where it tells us that it is okay to have 'good pride', but I believe it is implied in a number of ways. First of all, Jesus wants to say to us at the end of our life, "Well done good and faithful servant...." I believe he wants us to desire that commendation. That is, we can say to ourselves during our time on earth, and at the end of it. " I know I have not been perfect disciple of Jesus but I have done my best."

A sort of pride that is implied by Paul's words, which he wrote near the end of his life. "I have fought the fight and I have finished the race...."

There are other examples in the Bible, of a 'good pride'.. God said to Moses. I have chosen Bezalel....and I have filled him with the Spirit of God with *skill*, *ability* and *knowledge* in all kinds of crafts....to make artistic designs. Exod 31:1-4 (abrev)

This verse suggests that God is interested in his people using their skills, their abilities and their knowledge to do 'first class' work. That verse is very important because, Bezalel was not filled with the Spirit of God so he could be a first class, priest or prophet, but so he could be; a first class craftsman and designer. So there can be, good pride in work, well done.

Chapter 9

Humble Leaders

In the introduction, I posed the question

> "Is it possible to use all of our talents. Live life to the full. Enjoy life and other people. Face every challenge that life throws at us; and still at the same time, be humble?"

In the Bible, we read about leaders who were humble – yet who demonstrated that is was possible to be in a position of great power, authority and wealth. i.e. They are not exclusive states. Later in this chapter I provide some contemporary examples.

Four men who proved it was possible to have virtually unbridled power and yet remain humble, are. Joseph, David, Daniel and Peter.

Joseph

While they were living in Palestine, Joseph must have appeared to his older brothers 'big-headed' when he came to them and told them about a dream, and in the dream, they bowed down to him. Some time after Joseph told his older brothers about this dream, he came out to them in the country-side while they were looking after their flocks of sheep. As they were well away from their protective father, the brothers decided Joseph's appearance was a heaven-sent opportunity, to get rid of this, big-headed dreamer.

They had a quick discussion as he approached them, and decided to kill him; but because of the appeal by Joseph's nearest brother, Benjamin, they agreed to put him in a well. Later when some Ishmaelite traders were passing by who were on their way down to Egypt, they decided to sell him, as a slave. After arriving in Egypt he was sold as a slave, and then; despite serving his master faithfully, was falsely accused of rape. Because of that accusation, he was thrown into prison.

Events kept moving on, after that. He accurately interpreted a dream for one of his fellow prisoners, and because of that ability to interpret dreams; Joseph was eventually summoned to the Pharaoh's palace, because the Pharaoh also had a dream that he could not interpret. After Joseph interpreted the Pharaoh's dream, he was elevated to the position of the second most powerful man in Egypt and Joseph received - one of the most rapid promotions in history! He was promoted to a position we might call, today. The position of 'Vice-Pharaoh' or the 'Deputy-Pharaoh'.

What the Bible doesn't tell us, but archaeological excavations do - is that Joseph was given his own palace, near the Pharaoh's. This has been revealed as a result of the excavations by Professor Bitak, long time Professor of Egyptology at Vienna University. Over a thirty year period, Professor Bitak excavated a *Tel* which contained the palace of the Pharaoh, who ruled over Egypt at the time Joseph was there.

Professor Bitak, was surprised to find another palace nearby. After excavating that palace also, he concluded it was Joseph's palace because there was an elaborate tomb in the palace grounds; yet. Unlike many other tombs in Egypt; it had not been vandalised – and the tomb was completely empty. In the book of

Exodus, we read.

> "Moses took the bones of Joseph with him because Joseph had made the sons of Israel swear an oath. He said, God will surely come to your aid and then you must carry my bones up with you from this place. Exod 13:20

Professors Bitak's excavations of Joseph's palace, confirms what we read in Genesis. The account in Genesis implies that when Joseph's brothers came before him, they were in a significant building, like a palace - but it was not, the Pharaoh's palace. Consequently when we read about Joseph's brothers coming before Joseph and bowing down, it is very likely that it occurred, in Joseph's palace.

The other thing that is implicit in the story of Joseph's life, was that he went from being a prisoner with no rights; to the second most powerful man in Egypt with virtually unbridled powers, similar to those, of a dictator. In democratic countries, we find it hard to understand that rulers like Joseph, was answerable, only to the Pharaoh – and were not bound by any court or constitution or any other authority.

There was no free press in those times who

could send investigative reporters to write unfavourable reports about Joseph if he did something wrong or T.V channels who could send reporters to question him, if he acted harshly towards anybody (apart from those in the Pharaoh's household).

A number of years after Joseph was comfortably set up in his palace with his Egyptian wife; his brothers arrived. We know from the Bible's account, that initially he treated his brothers with a mixture of concern and testing. On their second journey to Egypt, and during their third audience with him, Joseph finally revealed himself, to them.

It must have come as a 'huge shock' ' to Joseph's brothers, to realise that the man standing before them, dressed like an Egyptian ruler – and the second most powerful man in Egypt, was their brother. But there was a far greater reason for the Bible telling us that they stood speechless before him (once he told them who he was); for they knew instantly that, *if* he had revenge on his mind; at that moment they were as good as, dead men.

Both they and Joseph knew they had committed one of the ultimate betrayals. They had sold one of their 'own' family members to foreigners, and once the money they received had been divided out amongst the eleven brothers, their share would not have been, very significant. So it wasn't as if they were making a huge amount of money out of the deal, when they sold him as a slave. It was purely a deal to get rid of a brother who was in their eyes. A dreaming/arrogant, family member.

When they sold Joseph to those traders, they would have anticipated that he would spend the rest of his days in Egypt, as a slave. Now, as they stood before him, they must have thought they were in a living nightmare – for their brother, sold for a modest sum, now had them in the palm of his hand, and was able to order any fate, he chose - with by a command and a wave of his hand.

As they stood before him this third time, they would have realised that on their first journey to Egypt, he had by-passed a very good opportunity to arrest and torture them to death, or at a minimum; make them slaves for the rest of their lives. They thought that during their second visit (when they again appeared before him to purchase grain), he had bypassed another very good opportunity to extract revenge.

Now as they stood before him a third time, they must have thought that Joseph had waited patiently for this time; and now (in a second of time) their fate would be sealed by the wave of a hand or a command to his aides. Constitutional rights, did not exist, as far as Joseph was concerned. Maybe a quick word in the ear of the Pharaoh about why he had tortured and executed these eleven men; but that was all that would have been necessary.

The type of instant power that was available to Joseph at that time; is illustrated by the way the Pharaoh acted. On a whim, he had his baker and wine-taster thrown into prison. Some time later during a party, and on another whim; he had them both brought before him. The wine-taster was restored to his position; and the baker executed. No courts or constitutional rights or free press to worry about – just a word from the Pharaoh, was all that was necessary.

So as the brothers stood before Joseph, speechless, they knew and he knew, that in a split second, at the wave of his hand and at his command, a similar fate, could await them

- as happened to the baker and wine-taster of the Pharaoh. When Joseph, to their surprise acted kindly towards his brothers and spoke in a way that had their future good in mind, it was a sign of Joseph's humility.

He knew well – and, had not forgotten - that it was 'God' who had arranged his elevation to the second most powerful position in Egypt. Among the words he said to them at this time were....

> do not be angry with yourselves for selling me here, because it was to save lives that God sent me ahead of you." Gen 45:5.

In the first chapter I made the point that most of what we have; is a gift. Our talents, time, possessions, position. That is how Joseph regarded his status. It was the result of God's plan, not because he was the best looking (though it is implied that Potiphar's wife thought he was, alright) or any other ability or attribute.

There is another observation that can be made about Joseph's humility, he 'continued' to acknowledge that it was God who had given him that leadership position. Years after his extended family had settled in Egypt, their father died; and the brothers became worried that, now their father was dead, surely Joseph no longer had any reason to continue to show kindness to them. But he said to them.

> "Don't be afraid. Am I in the place of God? You intended to harm me, but God intended it for good to accomplish what is now being done, the saving of many lives."
> Gen 45:19-20

Long before Jesus showed grace to many people, and taught about forgiving and blessing our enemies; Joseph showed grace to his brothers and their families, and continued to show grace. There is an element of the story of the prodigal son in this account of the brothers and Joseph. In the parable of the prodigal son, the son returns home; expecting condemnation; and hoping to be taken on as a servant. But he got welcomed and a party was thrown.

Likewise, in the story of Joseph and his brothers, they must have expected to be made slaves at a minimum, yet. Joseph wept over them, and hugged them, and gave them a generous supply of gifts and food; and a promise of much more care, if they brought their families to Egypt.

> Humble leaders acknowledge that it is God who has elevated them to power. They also acknowledge that their elevation is for a purpose.

Daniel

Daniel, like Joseph, was a man who was elevated to a high position in the court of King Nebuchadnezzar of Babylon. Daniel, like Joseph before him, had an ability to interpret dreams and like Joseph gave the credit to 'God', for his ability to interpret dreams. That became apparent during the reign of King Nebuchadnezzar's successor, King Belshazzar.

When Daniel was given the opportunity to interpret the writing that had appeared on a wall of the palace during a party, King Belshazzar became very frightened and ordered his astrologers to come and interpret the writing. They were unable to do so, but the queen; remembering how Daniel had interpreted dreams during the reign of Nebuchadnezzar, suggested that Daniel might be able to interpret the writing.

Daniel was so aware that it was 'God' who had given him the ability to interpretation of the writing on the wall (and it was not because of his own brilliance or insight) that he would not take any gifts from the king Belshazzar or accept the position of the third most powerful ruler in the kingdom, which the king offered him.

He told the king.

> "You may keep your gifts for yourself and give your rewards to someone else." Dan 5:17

> Humility towards God is not about who we are, but who God is.

There was another way in which Daniels humility is revealed. During the later reign of king Darius (who had overthrown Belshazzar), Daniel reviewed a prophecy of the prophet Jeremiah that; the exile in Babylon would be for a period of seventy years, and so he began to pray that God would help the Jewish people return to their land.

During the prayer Daniel prayed at that time, he confessed his own sins and those of his people. Daniel 9:20. His own sins? At one stage, those who were jealous of Daniel's position, tried very hard to find any fault in the way he handled his administrative responsibilities, but could not find any.

> "He was faithful, always responsible, and completely trustworthy." Dan 6:4 NLT

Even his enemies had to admit that he was a man who was, without fault or sin.

When the angel Gabriel came to him, he said to Daniel

> "you are very precious to God." (NLT) or "You are highly esteemed." (NIV) Dan 9:23.

So both God, and his enemies; considered Daniel and honest and trustworthy man. So if both God and his enemies considered Daniel, virtually faultless; why did he confess his sins?

There is a misconception about people who are close to God. That misconception is that people who are close to God; are so saintly - that they never commit any sins and they have no need to confess, any sins. That is one perspective. Another perspective is this.

People who are really close to God (and who live more godly and less sinful lives - than most Christians; confess their sins more, because they are close to God!

People who are close to God, realise that

though they may not be doing any of the obvious sins like: Cheating on their partner. Stealing from their employer. Lying, assault, murder e.t.a. When they come into the presence of God. . When they are still before him, some of the so-called, smaller sins* show up because they are in the presence of a totally holy God, in whom there is *no* darkness or dishonesty or selfishness or lust or greed.

In the presence of God's total and complete holiness, the words and actions; the thoughts and attitudes that we all, so easily justify – are shown to be sin. That is illustrated by the vision the prophet Isaiah had, of God on his throne. Prior to the vision, there is every reason to believe Isaiah led a, very godly life; both from Isaiah's own accounts and others accounts, e.g. 2nd Kings.

However, when he was in God's presence, Isaiah was so aware of God's holiness (6;3), and his sinfulness. 6:5 He said, "Its all over..." (NLT). Or the King James renders the same words "I am undone..."

Both phrases convey, the same idea. "Its all over..." means. "My self perception of being a good and godly man does not stack up when I am in the presence of a totally holy God."

There is another reason, people confess their sins; apart from being close to God. Another factor is their humility. They are humble and honest enough to admit they commit sins too. It is not just those who are committing, obvious sins. Humility and a willingness to confess our sinfulness, go hand in hand; just as pride and a denial of any wrong doing; go, hand in hand.

Humble people admit, they sin and are sinners; even though their sins; might be very minor; in most people's eyes. The Apostle Paul was like Daniel and like Isaiah. He wrote. "Christ Jesus came into the world to save sinners – of whom I am the worst." 1 Tim 1:15

Like the other two prophets, there is no reason to believe that Paul lived an exemplary life. He, more than any other Christian, helped shape; the Christian Church. I.e. About half of the books of the New Testament; were written by Paul. The Apostle Paul has become, with good reason; a saint in a number of denominations and a number of denominations have churches named, St Paul's.

So why did Paul write, I am the worst of sinners; when from both what he wrote and what others have written about his life (the latter part of the book of Acts written by Luke, and was focussed on Paul's life); he was a very godly man who lived what he taught. There are at least, 3 reasons why Paul wrote he was, "the worst of sinners."

- He was close to God.
- He was sensitive to the Holy Spirit, (the Spirit of truth) and when people are sensitive to the Spirit of truth; the Holy Spirit may gently put his finger on areas of our lives which (though outwardly are not major), but inhibit our walk with God and Jesus.
- He was humble and honest enough to admit he was a sinner – as in fact, we all are. C.f. Rom 3:23

People are willing to confess their sins when they are two things:

Both humble and honest.

It was only after David admitted the major sins of adultery (cheating) and murder that he wrote. "Surely you require truth in the inner parts....Psa 51:6 When we are honest with our self, we can admit that we too; are sinners.

David

King David was another humble leader. Before the people of Israel, he prayed these words.

> *"But who am I and who are my people,that we should be able to give as generously as this? Everything comes from you, and we have given you only what comes from your hand." 1 Chron 29:14 (N.I.V)*

David asked the question "who am I" That was not a question he should have asked, because. He was merely, Israel's most successful king and the borders of Israel grew to their greatest extent, during his reign. And like other rulers of the time; there were no checks on his power (like today; checks such as the free press and constitutional rights) and like other rulers of the time. All the taxes collected in the kingdom, came directly to him; making him; immensely wealthy! He would easily have been, by today's standards, a multi-billionaire. Yet this immensely wealthy all powerful king, acknowledged in prayer that, before God, 'everyone' including himself; was really; very small and insignificant and that. 'Everything' they had, had come from God. He also implied that it is their *privilege*; to give to back to God, what he had given.

Humble leadership is about acknowledging, that, before God the greatest Christian is really nothing (and it is only because of his amazing love and grace that we are, really something). Humble leadership also acknowledges that any possessions and wealth we have, ultimately come from God and that it is our privilege - to use those gifts/possessions/money for; the benefit of others and the kingdom of God.

Moving forward to the time of the Apostles, we find on Peter's lips; a similar humility to King David. Peter did not have wealth and secular power, like David, but spiritual power and the position of the most prominent Apostle in the Jerusalem Church. Something Jesus had groomed him for. Peter explained his attitude to spiritual power, one day, when he and John were walking through a Temple gate, and there was a crippled man there, begging for money. When the crippled man looked to Peter and John for money, Peter said to him.

> "Silver and gold I do not have, but
> what I have I give you. In the name
> of Jesus Christ of Nazareth, walk."
> Acts 3:6

After the man was healed and he began to cling to Peter. Many soon recognised this formerly crippled man, who walking and holding on to Peter, and concluded that a miracle must have occurred; so there was a commotion. Sensing that some wanted to give him, adulation as, a miracle worker; Peter said to them.

"Men of Israel, why does this surprise you? Why do you stare at us as if by our own power or godliness we made this man walk?..... It is Jesus name and the faith that comes through him that has given complete healing to him.... Acts 3:12&16

Joseph and Daniel recognised that their positions and ability to interpret dreams, had come from God. Peter emphasised at the time of the healing of this crippled man, was not because of his own power or godliness (another translation renders the words godliness as *goodness*), the healing occurred – it was because of his faith in the risen, Jesus.

Peter's attitude echo's that of Jesus. On one occasion during his ministry he sent the twelve out to drive out demons and heal the sick. Matt 10:1 Before he sent them out to do these miracles, he said to them. "Freely you have received, freely give." Matt 10:8

Like Joseph and like Peter, the Apostle Paul was another, very humble leader. We can see that from a number of statements he wrote.

> "Who am I and who is Apollos?" 1 Cor 3:5 (L.B)

> "I am not perfect yet, but I press on towards the goal..."

> "In grace He (Jesus) called me."

> "Now I know in part" 1 Cor 13:12

> "We are .... perplexed...." 2 Cor 4:8

Let's review, just a few of those statements by Paul.

Who am I and who is Apollos,... 1 Cor 3:5 (L.B)

That was a question Paul asked, when writing to the Christians at the Church at Corinth. The background to this question is that some in the Church were saying that they were followers of Peter, others of Apollos, others Paul; and others Christ.

In the first chapter of that first letter to the Christians at Corinth, Paul was trying to take himself out of the picture and put the focus on Jesus. He reminded the Christians there of his real purpose, which was

> "For Christ did not send me to baptize, but to preach the gospel – not with words of human wisdom, less the cross of Christ be emptied of its power. 1 Cor 1:17 (N.I.V)

Now I know in part" 1 Cor 13:12

Another amazing statement that Paul made, which also showed his humility, was this statement. "Now I know in part..." One would have thought that the person wrote nearly half of the books in the New Testament. The person who; more than any other person, shaped the New Testament Church, would not write. "Now I know in part" If any Christian since the time of Jesus, has the right to say."I know the faith, from A-Z" or. "I know, all there is to know about God and Jesus and this new faith", it was, Saul of Tarsus!

> *Humble people concentrate on their mission, and not their position.*

There is a common thread running through what Joseph said. What Daniel said and what Peter said. All three are acknowledging the role of the Father (in Josephs and Daniels case) or Jesus, in Peter and Paul's case. It was not their personality or looks or talents or godliness that got them to a point of being revered by others. It was God working through them so that the Father or Son could be glorified – and his purposes on earth; achieved. In all this, there must be a message for Christians and for Christian leaders today.

At one level, the success of any Church or Christian organisation or an organisation or business run by Christian leader/s, depends on having at the head, a gifted leader who uses his or her gifts well. Success also depends on having under them; the right people with the right talents appointed to the right positions – and on having an achievable vision for the organisation, along with prayer and hard work.

Even with

>The right leaders in place
>The Prayer
>The vision
>The most effective plan in place,

humble and godly leaders admit that the final result is not because all those obvious things are in place. The final word is:

>*"...the Lord has done this, and it is marvellous in our eyes. Psa 118:23*

For all of us there is a message from the examples of these leaders. It was noted in an earlier chapter about pride, that the middle letter of that word pride; is 'i'. *I* am better than you. *I* know more than you. *I* have more money than you. *I* have more power than you. *I* have done this ...... e.t.a. A proud person's life revolves around the word I - while the humble person's life revolves around three words, each of which have the letter 'e', in them. *Me, we* and *Thee*

Me.

Despite what I wrote about the letter 'i' being in the middle of the word pride. The Father/Son and Holy Spirit want to use you and I. Or we could say. He wants to use 'me'. Not a robot, but me, with my talents, experience, training. Faults and weaknesses. Who we are, is incredibly important to the Father/Son and Holy Spirit. They are looking for channels of his love. People like you and I. All they need is, people who are available.

We

However, for the humble person, life doesn't end at the borders of me. There are other people in our lives, who the humble person will acknowledge in any statement about. Where they are at and, what they have done.

The family we came from. The people at our schools, College or place of learning. People who, along the way who encouraged us or if necessary, corrected us. The people who support us now; in whatever we do. The Christians who have been an example to us.

During the London Olympics, two gold medallists were interviewed by a reporter; and asked about the reasons for their success. One of them took the opportunity while he was being interviewed; to thank his wife; and family and coach and others who had helped and supported him over the years.

Thee

Ok, *Thee,* is an old fashioned word for God. In this book, I am only using and old-fashioned word (*Thee)* because it is simpler to have the phrase. *Me, we* and *Thee.* The point has already been made earlier in this chapter, that humble leaders acknowledge that, it is God, who has given them the opportunity to rise to the positions they have obtained.

Going back to the recent Olympics in London; I noticed a number of athletes from a number of countries, pointing to the sky after they had run one of the fastest times in the world or jumped further than any other at the games;

or. Scored a brilliant goal; as if acknowledging that their talent (their talent to be a world beater); had come from God.

Humility is a very healing and freeing attitude to have. If along with honesty; we can be honest with

- Ourselves
- Others, and
- God or Jesus

that

- We have sinned. (do sin)
- Made a mistake (make mistakes)
- Don't always get guidance right.

All of those admissions are freeing, for they mean we don't have to be trapped into the self delusion that we are perfect, or always make, the right decisions.

> May the God who loves you, bless you and make you a blessing to others. May Jesus who called you to be like himself and called you to be, yourself; give you strength to love others be they, sinner or saints, whether they be ordinary or, extraordinary people! Then, at the end of your life, you will know that you have lived a life that will have fulfilled; God's highest hope for you

and Jesus will say. "Well done, my true disciple. Amen and amen."